Mysteries of the Microscopic World

Bruce E. Fleury, Ph.D.

THE
GREAT
COURSES®

PUBLISHED BY:

THE GREAT COURSES
Corporate Headquarters
4840 Westfields Boulevard, Suite 500
Chantilly, Virginia 20151-2299
Phone: 1-800-832-2412
Fax: 703-378-3819
www.thegreatcourses.com

Bruce E. Fleury, Ph.D.
Professor of the Practice, Department of
Ecology and Evolutionary Biology,
Tulane University

Professor Bruce Edward Fleury is Professor of the Practice in the Department of Ecology and Evolutionary Biology at Tulane University. He received his B.A. in Psychology and General Science from the University of Rochester in 1971 and his M.A. in Library, Media, and Information Studies in 1979 from the University of South Florida's library school. Dr. Fleury's career as a college reference librarian led him to Tulane in 1983, where he became head of the university library's Science and Engineering Division. While taking classes toward a master's degree in biology to enhance his subject skills as a librarian, he rediscovered his interest in the natural world. He received his M.S. in Biology in 1989 and his Ph.D. in Biology in 1996.

Dr. Fleury wrote his doctoral dissertation on the link between the explosive growth of colonial wading birds like herons, egrets, and ibises and the rise of the crawfish aquaculture industry. He teaches between 600 and 700 students a year, and his course offerings include ornithology, introductory general biology and environmental biology, the history of life, and evolution in human health and disease. He has authored numerous articles and newspaper columns, both popular and professional, and the reference book *Dinosaurs: A Guide to Research*.

Dr. Fleury has won several teaching awards and has appeared in *Who's Who among America's Teachers*. Between 2001 and 2003, the Tulane chapter of the Mortar Board National College Senior Honor Society awarded him twice for outstanding teaching. In 2008, he was a guest speaker at the Mortar Board Last Lecture Series, where favorite professors are invited to give a lecture as if it would be their last. He admits it was disconcerting to receive an official letter that begins, "Congratulations, you have been invited to present your Last Lecture at Tulane University."

Most recently, Dr. Fleury worked as a consultant for Warner Bros.' space epic *Green Lantern*, working on several classroom and laboratory scenes, and serving as a consulting xenobiologist on alien life in general. He reports that the movie business is an odd combination of Disneyland and the Department of Motor Vehicles.

Having grown up in the shadow of the Adirondack Mountains in upstate New York, Dr. Fleury admits he was always a student of the natural world, and only recently got around to making it official. He says, "As a child, I only wanted to be 2 things when I grew up (you can ask my mom)—a librarian and a teacher." He considers himself quite fortunate to have been both.

You can find Dr. Fleury's home page at: http://www.tulane.edu/~bfleury. It includes links to several of his humorous columns on life in the Big Easy and to the courses he is currently teaching. ■

Table of Contents

Table of Contents

Table of Contents

SUPPLEMENTAL MATERIAL

Mysteries of the Microscopic World

Scope:

This course will take you on a guided tour through an invisible realm—a hidden world as close as your fingertips and as unfamiliar as the bottom of the sea. Our lives are shaped and nurtured, and sometimes threatened by this world and its inhabitants: countless millions of microorganisms, creatures as alien to us as we are to a flea.

In this course, we follow the long path of our coevolution with our microbial friends and foes, starting with our descent from the trees on the prehistoric plains of Africa. The simple act of setting foot on solid ground exposed us to a wealth of new microscopic parasites. As we evolved from nomadic hunter-gatherers to settled agriculturalists, we changed the way we related to microbes and the ways in which they could relate to us. As we settled into permanent camps and began to grow crops, our populations grew, making us vulnerable to crowd diseases like plague, flu, and smallpox—great epidemics of the ancient world that claimed millions of lives.

One of the deadliest microbes of the ancient world was *Yersinia pestis*, the bubonic plague, which swept through Europe in the 14th century as the Black Death. We look at how a subtle weave of history, biology, and human behavior made us vulnerable to the plague and try to imagine living through such an epidemic with no idea why everyone around us is dying. Is it divine retribution? Perhaps it is caused by an imbalance of the bodily humors, or fluids; or perhaps a miasma, an invisible cloud of disease emanating from unhealthy habitats and people, is to blame. We review such early ideas about disease as we trace the rise of germ theory, the growing realization that diseases were caused by microorganisms.

In the second set of lectures, we contrast the strategies humans have evolved to defend ourselves against microbial invaders with the strategies that microbes have evolved for attacking us. We examine how the rise of civilization has altered our environment and how microbes have rapidly adapted to take advantage of those environmental changes, leading to diseases like Lyme, Legionnaire's, toxoplasmosis, and death by chocolate. We also look at the effects of natural environmental changes, such as an El Niño weather pattern, on microbes.

It's hard to imagine how tiny creatures like bacteria and viruses could cause such dramatic changes in the lives of large and powerful beings like ourselves, but we will consider 2 examples of how microbes may have altered the course of human history. We'll learn about hookworm, the so-called germ of laziness, which held back the economic development of the American South and may have cost it the Civil War, and the 1918 Flu, the worst epidemic in human history, which helped to set the stage for World War II.

In the third set of lectures, we roll up our sleeves and delve into the complexities of the immune system, our best protection against microscopic invaders. This knowledge will enable us to better appreciate the subtle and insidious strategy of the AIDS virus, which directly targets the immune system. We also explore the causes and consequences of autoimmune diseases like multiple sclerosis and lupus, when the body turns on itself and treats its own cells and tissues as if they were foreign invaders.

In the fourth set of lectures, we follow Christopher Columbus and the European explorers across the Atlantic Ocean and witness the devastation of New World native populations from the microbial hitchhikers they carried. Then we consider the possibility of another great microbial exchange as we prepare to cross the final frontier into outer space. What new forms of microscopic life might be waiting for us between the stars?

Finally, we see how microbes shaped the world in which we live by creating our oxygen atmosphere, by enriching the soil for plants to grow, and by opening an evolutionary pathway leading to the cells that make up our body. We consider the many ways in which microorganisms continue to make our world a healthier, tastier, and more profitable place in which to live. By the time we've completed our journey together, you will better understand the diverse ways in which microbes affect our lives and will have gained a deeper appreciation for the marvels and mysteries of the microscopic world. ■

The Invisible Realm
Lecture 1

There are roughly 100 trillion cells in the human body, but roughly 90 trillion of them—9 out of every 10—are different kinds of bacteria. These microorganisms do both good things and bad things for us and to us. We interact with microbes as competitors and companions, as predator and prey.

There are more **bacteria** in your mouth right now than the total number of men, women, and children that have ever existed on Earth since humans separated from the great apes some 6–10 million years ago. But individual **pathogens** are pretty fragile creatures. You can wipe out entire populations of bacteria with nothing more than a teaspoon of antibiotics.

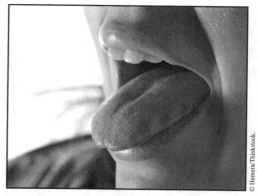

Even the cleanest human mouth is home to countless but fragile bacteria.

Along the journey from the plains of Africa to the towers of midtown Manhattan, we humans changed from nomadic hunter-gatherers to settled farmers—a change that forever altered our relationship to the microbial world. As we built great cities, dense urban populations triggered the great plagues of antiquity.

For centuries we've been engaged in an evolutionary arms race with an invisible foe. Microbes have evolved strategies to invade and exploit us, including resistance to our most powerful antibiotics, just as we've evolved ways to fight back, including our complex immune system.

Not all microbes are pathogens; some are essential to our health and welfare: They created the air that we breathe; they created the type of cells that make up our bodies. Frankly, we'd be hard-pressed to survive without them.

Will we ever reach a balance where both man and microbe can safely coexist? Probably not. Bacteria evolve much more rapidly than we do because they can exchange genetic information in little snippets called **plasmids**, without that lengthy and often messy process of sperm meeting egg.

Modern ecologists have learned to appreciate that nature is often not in balance.

The idea that nature keeps itself in balance isn't new; it is at least as old as the golden age of Greek philosophy. In fact, the original meaning of "evolution"—from the Latin *evolutio*, meaning "to unroll; to unfold"—was the unfolding of the divine plan for nature. Many theologians thought that the balance of nature was the most eloquent argument you could make to prove the divine plan and worried—as Darwin did—about the cosmic forces that preserved that delicate balance between organism and environment.

How can a mere 6 billion humans hope to prevail against countless trillions of microbes? To answer that question, we need to understand the ways populations are controlled and regulated by their interactions with other organisms and with the Earth. These **extrinsic limiting factors** include sunlight, water, nutrients, food supply, competitors, predators, and availability of symbiotic partners.

Modern ecologists have learned to appreciate that nature is often not in balance. Ecosystems are frequently disturbed by forces like storms, fires, floods, hungry animals, and diseases. These ecosystems adapted so well to disturbance that they often come to rely on it—a phenomenon ecologists call **nonequilibrium theory**.

Humans are subject to the same fundamental laws of nature as other organisms; we have to compete with one another, and with other species, for the limited resources that we need to survive. Two species can't peacefully coexist if they both need the same essential limiting resource. If one species is a better competitor than another, it might even eliminate its rival altogether—what we call **competitive exclusion**.

Competition can be intraspecific (between members of the same species), or it can be interspecific (between members of different species). Intraspecific competition is more intense because each organism's needs almost exactly match the needs of other members of its species; they share the same ecological **niche**.

Microorganisms like bacteria are so amazingly small that they actually live in a very different physical universe from us. They're buffeted by microscopic physical and chemical forces in ways that are hard for us to even appreciate.

Most microorganisms are so small they don't need specialized biological equipment to exchange gases, get rid of wastes, or move chemicals through their cells. The ability of microbes to sense the presence of food or danger depends on their ability to sense the concentration gradient of certain molecules, and to orient themselves and navigate accordingly.

Microbes accomplish all these chores and more through **diffusion**. Due to their small size, bacteria have a relatively large surface area for diffusion. As objects get smaller, they have relatively less volume—less interior—with respect to surface area. This greatly enhances their ability to rely on diffusion. ∎

Important Terms

bacteria (sing. **bacterium**): Primitive unicellular organisms; when capitalized, refers to one of the 3 taxonomic domains of living things.

competitive exclusion: A situation in which one species or population outcompetes its rival to the point where the rival is locally eliminated.

diffusion: The movement of atoms and molecules from an area of higher concentration to an area of lower concentration.

extrinsic limiting factor: A limiting factor that comes from outside the individual or population, such as sunlight, water, or nutrients.

niche: The functional role that an organism plays in an ecosystem; also, the sum total of a species's needs and the range of conditions within which it can survive.

nonequilibrium theory: The idea that certain ecosystems are not harmed by disturbance but rather thrive on it.

pathogen: The umbrella term for disease-causing organisms, including bacteria, viruses, flukes, and nematode worms, and so forth.

plasmid: Tiny loops of genes freely exchanged between bacteria, often bearing useful traits.

Suggested Reading

Crawford, *The Invisible Enemy*.

Dobson, *Disease*.

Questions to Consider

1. How does the original meaning of the word "evolution" (from the Latin *evolutio*) reflect the way pre-Darwinian scholars saw the natural world?

2. In what way, mathematically speaking, is small size an advantage for a single-celled organism like a bacterium?

Stone Knives to Iron Plows
Lecture 2

As humans changed the way we lived and consequently changed our environment, microbes had to adapt or perish. In many ways, these changes left us vulnerable to a host of new microbial invaders and new microbial strategies.

Plagues were not always a problem for humankind. **Epidemics** couldn't spread very far when we lived in scattered nomadic tribes, but when we started gathering together to build villages, raise crops, and domesticate animals, we changed our niche and altered our habitat.

About 4 to 7 million years ago, vast ice sheets began to spread over North America and Eurasia. The tropical African climate became much cooler and drier. This new environment favored creatures such as our distant ancestor *Australopithecus*, who could live in the trees yet still cross the open grasslands to forage. But contact with the ground meant contact with an entirely new group of microbes.

Why didn't all these new pathogens wipe out our distant ancestors? What probably saved us was our small population size. Humans lived in nomadic bands of 1–2 dozen individuals, perhaps fewer. Bands rarely crossed paths and were never in one place long enough to pollute the area. The occasional disease outbreak was self-limiting; once the disease had burned through the tribe, it had nowhere to go. Only diseases carried by insects and animals or diseases able to persist in the soil would have caused any serious problems for early man.

The human population made a sudden leap from 7 or 8 million people in 10,000 B.C. to about 100 million by 5000 B.C. This Neolithic population boom probably marks humanity's transition to a radically different lifestyle, from nomadic hunting and gathering to settled agriculture.

The agricultural revolution allowed us to build up large urban settlements that would not only become the basis for the great civilizations of antiquity and the nodes in a vast web of trade; they also served as a breeding ground and transit network for many of our worst microbial foes. Food storage, water and soil contamination, deforestation, and accumulation of personal possessions all provided new environments for disease, especially those carried by insects and rodents.

About 6000 years ago, human population density became high enough for 2 entirely new types of population regulation to kick in: **density-dependent limiting factors**, factors related to the intensity of the competition for limited resources, and **intrinsic limiting factors**, changes in an individual's reproductive physiology or behavior that reduce population size.

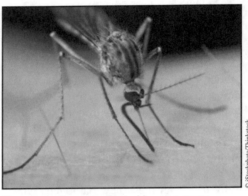
© iStockphoto/Thinkstock.

Disease cycles are affected by numerous factors, including the presence of vector organisms, like mosquitos.

The results of urbanization were measles, smallpox, typhus, plague, syphilis, scarlet fever—a long and growing list of epidemic diseases that would shape the entirety of human history. For example, Thucydides wrote what may be the first description of a **pandemic** in his *History of the Peloponnesian War*. No one knows what microbe was responsible for this plague, but it devastated the Athenian army and citizenry and contributed to the end of the golden age of Greek civilization.

It's no accident that epidemic diseases seem to wax and wane throughout history. Many microbes can't survive for long outside of a human body. An epidemic disease will infect everybody in the population in a relatively short period of time, and the victims either die or recover and have **immunity**. The pattern that results from all this is a series of population cycles between host and pathogen. The microbe quickly uses up all its available hosts, and has to travel to another population to survive.

Disease cycles can be very complex. They are affected by political, economic, and climactic factors. They can even be affected by the presence of other diseases; tuberculosis, for example, was nearly eradicated by the end of the 20th century, but the spread of HIV/AIDS gave the disease a new set of vulnerable hosts to infect.

Today, the world's population stands at over 6 billion and is rapidly increasing. By 2025 we could be near 8.5 billion people; India alone could have 600 million more people, Nigeria 200 million more people, and China 357 million more people. Our growing population will have a tremendous effect on the environment, creating a wealth of new opportunities for microorganisms. ■

Important Terms

density-dependent limiting factor: A limiting factor whose effects are directly proportional to the density of a population, such as predation or disease.

epidemic: An outbreak of disease that exceeds the expected norm, usually applied to an infectious disease that appears suddenly and moves rapidly through a population.

immunity: Disease resistance acquired by exposure to a pathogen. The immune system "remembers" the encounter by keeping some antibodies around from each disease it defeats, in case the same pathogen returns.

intrinsic limiting factor: A limiting factor that operates from within the individuals of a population, affecting reproductive physiology or reproductive behavior.

pandemic: An epidemic that occurs over a wide geographic area.

Suggested Reading

Crawford, *Deadly Companions*.

Karlen, *Man and Microbes*.

McNeill, *Plagues and Peoples*.

Questions to Consider

1. How is immunity different from genetic resistance?

2. Why were epidemic diseases not a big problem for early human populations of hunter-gatherers?

The Angel of Death
Lecture 3

The Medieval Warm Period allowed for a rapid increase in European population, but the following Little Ice Age led to a collapse in agriculture, leading to generations of famine and malnutrition, and helped to make medieval Europe especially vulnerable to the deadly clutches of the Black Death.

Many of the most devastating epidemics come from **vector**-borne diseases, like typhus, malaria, and dengue fever. A vector is any organism that carries a microbe that causes a disease. Most vector-borne diseases are carried by arthropods—flies, fleas, ticks, lice, and mosquitoes, and some rely on multiple vectors. Unlike crowd-borne diseases, they have no difficulty surviving without secondary hosts.

Between A.D. 950 and A.D. 1250, Europe basked in one of the most fruitful, productive, and disease-free periods in its history, the **Medieval Warm Period**. But this warm spell was followed by an extended period of damp, chilly weather called the **Little Ice Age**, which lasted from about 1350 to about 1850.

Symptoms of the coming climate shift were evident by the early 14th century; summers in northern Europe became too cool and damp for grain to fully ripen, leading to the **Great Famine** (1315–1317). Severe storms, floods, and droughts became more frequent as the Little Ice Age set in, and it became harder and harder to grow crops. Millions starved; thousands of villages simply disappeared. Social and political structures broke down.

Into this already dismal period came the Black Death, a pandemic that would kill half the remaining population of Europe. Caused by an ancient vector-borne microbe carried by oriental rat fleas, this particular outbreak began in Central Asia or China around 1320–1340, then spread to India and Africa along the Silk Road. Italian soldiers who were exposed to the microbe during the Siege of Caffa in the Crimea brought it to Sicily and then mainland Europe. The disease reached Britain, its furthest port of call, in 1348.

Weakened by generations of famine and crowded into cities fouled by garbage, sewage, and rats, European populations were sitting ducks for the Black Death. Populations fell 40–60 percent, with up to 75–100 million dead in the 14th century alone. The plague ebbed and flowed throughout Europe for the next 300 years.

There are 3 distinct forms of plague: bubonic, pneumonic, and septicemic. Modern antibiotics and modern **vaccines** are effective against all 3.

Black rats are hosts for oriental rat fleas, which in turn are hosts for the Black Death.

- Bubonic plague is a disease of the lymphatic system with flu-like symptoms, followed by swelling of the lymph glands, delirium, convulsions, coma, and often death—about 40–60 percent mortality in 2–8 days if left untreated.

- In pneumonic plague, the disease spreads to the lungs and can then be spread through coughing and sneezing. Additional symptoms include coughing up blood, progressive pneumonia, and shock. The fatality rate is over 90 percent, and death occurs in as little as 1–2 days.

- In septicemic plague, the bacterium enters the bloodstream, where a bacterial toxin interferes with clotting. Victims quickly bleed to death internally. It kills virtually 100 percent of its victims, most of them in less than a day.

Successive waves of Black Death struck the Old World over the centuries. A pandemic that began in China around 1890 has since claimed 15 million lives and finally circled the globe, entering the United States through Chinese workers in San Francisco. By that time, however, we were aware of germ theory and were eager to hunt down this ancient enemy.

A Swiss-born, Paris-based doctor named Alexandre Yersin went to Hong Kong in 1894 to investigate the disease. Working in a primitive grass hut laboratory because the British authorities would not let him use their state-of-the-art hospitals, he identified and isolated the bacterium *Pasteurella pestis*, later renamed *Yersinia pestis* in his honor, and determined that it was carried by black rats. Then Paul-Louis Simond, a French colonial army doctor, proved that it was the bite of the oriental rat flea, *Xenopsylla cheopis*, that transmitted the infection from host to host.

> **Weakened by generations of famine and crowded into cities fouled by garbage, sewage, and rats, European populations were sitting ducks for the Black Death.**

The pandemic that began in 1890 is still going on today but has been relatively mild. Several cases of plague are reported every year worldwide, but it never spreads very far. Part of the reason may be that rats are scarcer than they used to be. Today's rats are also more domesticated; they tend to stay in one house or one neighborhood, so the plague never spreads beyond the local rodent population. ∎

Important Terms

Great Famine: A famine in Europe between A.D. 1315 and 1317 that claimed millions of lives.

Little Ice Age: A 500-year climate aberration (A.D. 1350–1850) during which temperatures in Europe were significantly colder than normal; the period was characterized by extreme and intense weather, such as floods and droughts.

Medieval Warm Period: A climate aberration preceding the Little Ice Age, during which average temperatures were significantly higher than normal.

vaccine: A therapeutic technique that introduces foreign antigens into an animal to help improve immune response to a particular pathogen; usually made from dead microbes, fragments of dead microbes, or microbial toxins.

vector: Any organism that carries a pathogen.

Suggested Reading

Gottfried, *The Black Death*.

Scott and Duncan, *Return of the Black Death*.

Tuchman, *A Distant Mirror*.

Ziegler, *The Black Death*.

Questions to Consider

1. Why have some biologists suggested that the Black Death and the bubonic plague are different diseases?

2. Bubonic plague is very much alive and well and living in the American Southwest. Why do you rarely hear of an outbreak of plague in modern times?

Germ Theory
Lecture 4

Before we could begin to solve the puzzle of disease, we first had to realize that diseases were caused by tiny little creatures feeding on our bodies. With the realization that microbes were the cause of human diseases came a growing awareness that we were engaged in an ongoing evolutionary struggle with these microscopic creatures.

In the days before the invention of the microscope, before the rise of modern medicine, the common explanations for epidemics involved cosmic forces beyond human control, the whims of gods and demons, or simple astrological fate. More earthly-minded theorists blamed an imbalance of bodily fluids called the **humors**—black bile, yellow bile, phlegm, and blood. Still others blamed a **miasma**—bad air.

All these ideas might sound foolish, but up until the late 17th century, no one on Earth had ever actually seen a **microbe**—creatures so small, we have to measure them in microns (thousandths of a millimeter). Typical bacteria are only about 0.2–5 microns across.

Girolamo Fracastoro—a Renaissance doctor, mathematician, astronomer, geographer, and poet—suggested in *On Contagion and Contagious Diseases* (1546) that diseases were caused by tiny spores that could be spread by contact. But Fracastoro was too far ahead of his time, and his ideas faded away. In 1683, Antony van Leeuwenhoek was the first to use a microscope to observe the tiny creatures of the microbial world. But Leeuwenhoek didn't connect microorganisms to disease or to decay.

Louis Pasteur convinced the scientific world of the importance of microbes.

© Photos.com/Thinkstock.

The **germ theory** of disease wasn't accepted until the late 19th century. Louis Pasteur was the first to prove that wine **fermentation** was caused by a living organism, the yeast *Saccharomyces cerevisiae*. Along the way, he also saw other microorganisms in wine, beer, and vinegar. He concluded that different microbes could have different effects.

John Tyndall and Joseph Lister studied Pasteur's results and concluded that microbes must also be the cause of human diseases, but it fell to Robert Koch to firmly establish germ theory in the 1870s. Koch connected anthrax, tuberculosis, and cholera to specific bacteria. Seeking to tell bacteria apart and how to tell the beneficial ones from the dangerous ones, Koch also invented the agar plate for culturing bacteria that is still used in modern laboratories.

Koch's **postulates** are a series of steps to prove which specific microbe is causing a particular disease: (1) The bacteria must be present in every case of the disease; (2) it must be isolated and cultured from an infected person; (3) injecting the cultured bacteria into a healthy host must cause the disease; and (4) one must be able to recover the bacteria from the newly infected host.

Ignaz Semmelweis was a germ theory pioneer who paid a huge price for his efforts to fight puerperal (childbed) fever. In 1846, he was appointed assistant to the professor of the maternity clinic at the Vienna General Hospital. When one of his male medical colleagues died a few days after pricking his finger during an autopsy on a young mother, the colleague's body was riddled with the same type of damage seen in victims of childbed fever.

Semmelweis realized the connection: Medical students were going straight from performing autopsies to assisting at births, unintentionally spreading the disease. He was able to show that the death rate among new mothers was much, much lower if doctors and nurses washed their hands with chlorinated lime between patients. Sadly, rather than thank Semmelweis for his discovery, the medical community shunned him, and his boss fired him for suggesting that doctors and medical students were killing patients.

Despite all Semmelweis's efforts, doctors who don't wash their hands are still a problem today. Around 2 million hospitalized people every year acquire infections that are due to doctors and nurses who don't wash their hands. ∎

Important Terms

fermentation: An ancient metabolic pathway evolved by cells before the formation of an oxygen atmosphere. Fermentation produces alcohol as a byproduct.

germ theory: The theory that microorganisms were the cause of human diseases, finally established in the late 19th century.

humors: Bodily fluids whose imbalance was once thought to be the cause of human diseases. The 4 humors were black bile, yellow bile, phlegm, and blood. The theory of humors was inspired by the 4 elements of the ancient Greeks (earth, air, fire, and water).

Koch's postulates: A series of steps established by physician Robert Koch to prove that a particular microbe causes a particular disease.

miasma: A noxious vapor once believed to be the cause of human disease.

microbe: Any organism small enough to require a microscope to clearly see it.

Suggested Reading

De Kruif, *Microbe Hunters*.

Nuland, *The Doctors' Plague.*

Waller, *The Discovery of the Germ.*

1. What were some of the ways people explained infectious diseases before we discovered the microscopic world? Can you think of an alternate explanation not covered in the lecture?

2. Why, according to the medical theory of humors, was there no such thing as a specific disease?

Lecture 4: Germ Theory

The Evolutionary Arms Race
Lecture 5

Leigh Van Valen's Red Queen hypothesis states that organisms are doomed to extinction if they can't evolve apace with the organisms they interact with. He argues that genetic variation by definition is finite but the environment never stops changing, so sooner or later every species fails to keep up.

Microbes and humans are locked in a perpetual evolutionary arms race, a cycle of **coevolution** wherein each change in one organism leads to an evolutionary change in the other, advantage for advantage. Even our ultimate weapons, penicillin and **antibiotics**, have only driven microbes to greater evolutionary extremes.

Although Sir Alexander Fleming is usually credited with discovering penicillin in 1928, Ernest Duchesne, a French medical student, was the first to document the connection between *Penicillium* molds and healing in 1897. His research was inspired by noticing that the Arab stable boys at the French army hospital stables intentionally stored saddles in damp, dark rooms to encourage mold growth, which they knew promoted the healing of saddle sores.

Even earlier, the Roman scholar Pliny the Elder recommended using mushrooms to treat wounds. The ancient Egyptians used beer and bread therapeutically; the brewing and baking methods they used caused the development of tetracycline in the final product. But Duchesne was the first person to conduct true scientific experiments on mold's medicinal properties and the first to publish his results.

Penicillin turned out to be a very effective killer. It doesn't actually kill bacteria outright; it keeps them from reproducing, which amounts to the same thing in the long term.

Mass production of penicillin began in the last days of World War II, but producing penicillin in large quantities turned out to be a major challenge.

Some strains were more effective and more productive than others. *Penicillium chrysogenum*, discovered by lab technician Mary Hunt at a U.S. Department of Agriculture lab, turned out to have the best combination of effectiveness and ease of production.

Penicillin was soon followed by a host of other new wonder drugs. Gerhard Domagk discovered Prontosil, the first sulfa drug, in 1935. In 1943, Selman Waksman isolated streptomycin from soil bacteria, receiving the 1952 Nobel Prize for his efforts. Tetracyclines were isolated from *Streptomyces* soil bacteria in 1945 and a synthetic form patented in 1955.

But bacteria quickly evolved into strains resistant to tetracycline and every new antibiotic that we could invent, including, unfortunately, penicillin. Antibiotics are becoming less and less effective against more and more diseases. By the late 1980s, **antibiotic resistance** had reached alarming proportions, and multiple drug resistant (MDR) and extensively drug resistant (XDR) strains appeared. Methicillin-resistant *Staphylococcus aureus* (MRSA) alone is responsible for 17,000—18,000 deaths or more per year.

Bacteria can evolve resistance to antibiotics in several ways: a change in the permeability of their cell walls; disguising themselves by altering the surface of their cell membranes; altering the binding site the drug usually attaches to; or developing a bacterial enzyme to neutralize the drug. All of these changes are inheritable, and bacteria evolve 1000 times faster than we do.

One of the secrets of bacterial success is conjugation—the exchange of plasmids that code for a particular trait, like resistance to an antibiotic. A plasmid evolved by any one bacterium can soon be passed to billions of others; each bacterium can have several hundred copies of each plasmid, and with a little help from us, plasmids can be carried around the globe in a matter of hours.

Interestingly, fungi like *Penicillium* and bacteria like *Streptomyces* didn't evolve their antibiotic properties from their war against us; these properties evolved from their continual war with one another. Microbes have been competing with one another for billions and billions of years, yielding some very exotic and very effective chemical weapons.

The constant game of evolutionary one-upmanship is not only frightening; it is also costly. By the 1980s, resistant strains of bacteria were costing hospitals $30 billion per year because only the newest, most powerful, and therefore most expensive drugs have a hope of treating MDR and XDR infections. Meanwhile, a large share of the world's population simply can't afford treatment, so the bacteria spread on and on.

> **The constant game of evolutionary one-upmanship is not only frightening; it is also costly.**

The hidden cost of antibiotics is that they are completely indiscriminate killers of bacteria. They kill the normal bacterial symbionts—helpful (**mutualistic**) or neutral (**commensal**) strains—that live inside of us. Killing the helpful and neutral strains gives the harmful (**parasitic**) strains more freedom to do their worst.

What lessons can we learn from antibiotic resistance? Doctors should limit antibiotic use whenever possible; shouldn't prescribe antibiotics unless they know what the disease is; and should break up prescription patterns to avoid constant selection pressure on any one drug; Patients must use the full dosage prescribed to completely kill the bacteria. Farmers should stop feeding massive amounts of **prophylactic antibiotics** to healthy cattle and poultry. Finally, the medical industry should retire certain antibiotics altogether to allow vulnerable, treatable strains to reemerge and compete with the MDR and XDR strains. ∎

Important Terms

antibiotic: Any substance that either kills microbes outright or slows down their population growth.

antibiotic resistance: The evolutionarily acquired ability of microbes to either neutralize or withstand an antibiotic.

coevolution: An evolutionary change in one organism that leads to an evolutionary change in another organism that interacts with it.

commensalism: A form of symbiosis in which one partner is helped and the other is neither helped nor hindered, such as Spanish moss hanging on trees.

mutualism: A form of symbiosis in which both partners are helped by the relationship (the traditional meaning of symbiosis), such as a lichen, a fungus cooperating with a green algae or cyanobacteria.

parasitism: A form of symbiosis in which one partner is helped and the other is harmed.

prophylactic antibiotic: Antibiotics given without a clear indication of disease as a preventative measure.

Red Queen hypothesis: Theory of biologist Leigh Van Valen that there is an upper limit to adaptation. The genetic resources of any species are finite, and because the environment never stops changing, every species will eventually exhaust its ability to adapt to those changes and will go extinct.

Suggested Reading

Lappé, *Evolutionary Medicine.*

Spellberg, *Rising Plague.*

Questions to Consider

1. How does the prescription of prophylactic antibiotics promote bacterial resistance?

2. Why should you always finish the antibiotics the doctor prescribes for you to the last disgusting drop, even if you already feel better?

Microbial Strategies

Lecture 6

Both sides in the war between humans and microbes have evolved many strategies of attack and defense. Humans' strategies are avoiding exposure to microbes, keeping microbes out of the body, and destroying microbes that do get in. Microbes' strategies are to evade the host's defenses; attack the host's defenses; and change the host's behavior to benefit itself.

One of the most important microbial strategies is one of the easiest to overlook: their innate ability to make a lot more of themselves in a very short period of time. Some bacteria can divide as often as once every 20 minutes. At that rate, the offspring of a single bacterium in just 2 days would outnumber the entire human race—and that includes everyone who has ever lived.

This staggering reproductive output is critical for microorganisms because they live in a very perilous world. Almost everything we do, great or small, in the course of our everyday lives destroys thousands upon thousands of microbes. Bacteria and other microbes are therefore called r-selected species—species that rely on rapid reproduction for survival.

Human beings—and large vertebrates in general—are called K-selected species. K stands for carrying capacity—how many individuals of a species can be sustained by a given environment. K-selected species are adapted to stable or predictable environments; r-selected species, like microbes, are much better adapted to unstable or ephemeral environments. If its species is going to survive, it needs a way to move from one environment (or person) to the next.

Just as microbes have evolved a wide variety of strategies to attack us and exploit us, we've coevolved an equally impressive array of strategies to keep them at bay, like fever. The body's thermostat goes up a few degrees, just enough to kill the invading bacteria or **virus**. But fever comes with a price.

High fevers can lead to hallucinations, delirium, permanent organ and tissue damage, and even death.

Iron is an essential nutrient for both humans and bacteria, so humans have developed various strategies for **iron withholding**. When we're sick, we often develop strong aversion to iron-rich foods. Human breast milk is rich in an iron-binding protein called lactoferrin, which helps breast-fed babies fight off infection by starving invading bacteria.

Skin is humans' first line of defense in keeping microbes out of the body, a mechanical and chemical barrier against infections. Next, receptors on our tongues and in our stomachs

Bacteria need a steady supply of iron to survive. Avoid iron supplements and iron-rich foods when you have a bacterial infection.

are hard-wired to detect certain toxins; if we do eat something that's bad for us, we get rid of it as quickly as possible. Finally, if microbes breach our defenses, our immune systems flag them for destruction.

One strategy microbes use to thwart our immune system is to adopt a secret identity. Under normal circumstances, a cell can take a piece of an invading microbe and stick it on its exterior like a little flag to let the immune system know it has been invaded. Adenoviruses, a common cause of colds and sore throats, make a protein that interferes with the host cell's ability to make these cellular flags, so the infected cells become safe houses for the virus. The rabies virus attaches nerve cell receptors; the immune system thinks the virus is a neurotransmitter molecule and leaves it alone. African sleeping sickness, caused by protozoan called *Trypanosoma brucei*, changes its surface proteins every 9 days, so the immune system loses track of it.

Some microbes use the direct approach to breach our defenses: Streptococcus kills **white blood cells** outright. HIV, the human immunodeficiency virus, goes for helper T cells, killing the heart of the immune system.

The most intriguing microbial attack strategy of all is **host manipulation**. *Y. pestis*, which causes the bubonic plague, makes infected fleas ravenous so they bite harder and regurgitate concentrated wads of bacteria into their victims. Rabies invades the neurological system and causes aggression in its host, leading the host to bite and pass the rabies virus on.

Vector microbes, like the bubonic plague, use an intermediate organism to disperse themselves and infect new hosts. Although this can be an effective strategy for wide and rapid spread, the more links in a microbe's dispersal chain, the more things can go wrong. ■

Important Terms

host manipulation: A microbial strategy in which the parasite alters host behavior in a way that significantly benefits the parasite.

iron withholding: Adaptive response in which the human body sequesters or binds iron so that it is not accessible to bacteria, for whom it is a limiting nutrient.

virus: A microscopic organism consisting of a core of RNA or DNA in a protein capsule, which can only reproduce by invading a living cell and using its protein synthesis mechanisms to make and assemble copies of the virus.

white blood cell (a.k.a. **leukocyte**): An immune system cell that helps fight infectious diseases or foreign proteins. The presence and number of these cells is often used in the diagnosis of disease. White blood cell types include neutrophils, dendritic cells, lymphocytes, and macrophages.

Suggested Reading

Finlay, "The Art of Bacterial Warfare."

Nesse and Williams, *Why we Get Sick*.

Questions to Consider

1. What's the medical wisdom in the old folk saying "feed a cold, starve a fever"?

2. How is it possible to drive a parasite into extinction without actually killing all of them?

Virulence
Lecture 7

The vector strategy, despite its hazards, is a clear winner in the war between microbe and host. Vector-borne diseases are so virulent because as long as the vector population is doing well, the microbe does well. This suggests a strategy to tame such diseases: Isolate the vectors from the hosts.

Cooperation and coexistence often prevail in nature, thanks to coevolution. But if nature tends towards peaceful coexistence, then why do so many infectious diseases like cholera, malaria, and anthrax continue to be so virulent?

Competition and coevolution can cause some diseases to gradually lose their sting. Other diseases seem to come out of nowhere, ravage the world, and then disappear as mysteriously as they arose. Diseases ebb and flow for many reasons, but we can tease out some interesting patterns: Successful organisms find a balance over time with their competitors.

Imagine a new species of bacteria, an effective and **virulent** killer—in clinical terms, "virulent" means it kills a large percentage of its victims. But killing an entire population of hosts isn't a good long-term strategy; the microbe needs some hosts to survive and make contact with a fresh population of victims. Logic suggests that pathogens should coevolve with their hosts to become more **benign strains**, and with many diseases, like syphilis and scarlet fever, that's exactly what has happened.

How can we use our knowledge of competition, predation, and coevolution tip the balance of the evolutionary arms race in our favor? One effective strategy is the virulence antigen strategy: using targeted drugs and vaccines, rather than a broad-spectrum attack, to target virulent strains and leave more benign ones to fill the niche. Instead of trying to wipe out a microbe altogether, we need to focus our efforts on targeting those precise virulence factors that are unique to the bad strains but are not found in the more benign strains.

Another important aspect of virulence is dispersal. Getting into a victim is only half the battle; unless the microbe can escape to infect another victim, every host is going to be a dead end. If the microbe is too virulent, dispersal is sharply limited because nobody is left standing to spread it around.

With vector-borne diseases, however, an immobile host is less of a problem. In malaria, for example, semicomatose victims can't wave off the mosquitoes that feed on them and spread the disease to other hosts. Therefore, vector-borne diseases can be more virulent than diseases that rely solely on physical contact. In fact, diseases that are spread by contact often evolve to become less virulent, while vector-borne diseases can evolve toward more virulence.

Diseases that are spread by contact often evolve to become less virulent, while vector-borne diseases can evolve toward more virulence.

Direct transmission does have a few advantages; it doesn't rely on intermediate hosts. It doesn't expose the microbe to risks while getting from the vector to the host and back again. It is the strategy of choice in dense human populations. Life is tougher for vector-borne diseases; they face risks during vector-host and host-vector journeys. There are more links in the chain and hence a greater risk of failure. But the advantage for vector-borne diseases is that they can immobilize or kill a host with relative impunity.

Some diseases, like cholera and anthrax, are highly virulent but aren't carried by vectors. These diseases can enter the water supply, most commonly through human waste and through washing or disposing of contaminated bedding and clothing. Water takes over the role of the vector, so the virulence of water-borne disease can remain high.

Similarly, **nosocomial infections**—that is, hospital infections like childbed fever before the 20th century and MRSA today—can spread from one immobile patient to another through direct contact with nurses, doctors, other patients, and so on. Other people become the vectors.

Lecture 7: Virulence

Pathogens like anthrax that are more durable—ones that can survive outside a host for a significant period of time—can also be much, much more virulent than more mobile but less sturdy microbes.

Understanding the nature of vector-borne diseases suggests a very basic strategy to tame them: Simply make it more difficult for the vector to reach the host. Virulent strains are competing with more benign strains of their own and related species; anything that slows down the vector should tip the competitive balance in favor of the more benign strains. But microbial strategies are adaptations to a shifting landscape. That's the nature of evolutionary adaptation: It's always responding to a never-ending series of environmental changes. ∎

Important Terms

benign strain: A species or subspecies of microbe that is less harmful than competing strains of the same species.

nosocomial infection: A hospital-acquired infection.

virulence: The intensity of a particular infectious disease as measured by its mortality rate.

Suggested Reading

Ewald, *Evolution of Infectious Disease.*

Gluckman, Beedle, and Hanson, *Principles of Evolutionary Medicine.*

Infectious Disease: A Scientific American Reader.

Questions to Consider

1. What do a hospital worker, a mosquito, and a river all have in common?

2. Why is high virulence an evolutionary trade off for a microorganism?

Death by Chocolate
Lecture 8

Human civilization gave microbes countless new dispersal routes, from highways to hypodermic needles, and new habitats, from kitty litter to air conditioning. Agriculture in particular has led to ecosystem disturbance and increased human contact with opportunistic microbes.

The trade routes and roads of antiquity were interstate highways for microbes, taking them from populations with **herd immunity** to new, **naïve populations**. The movement of bubonic plague from East to West and smallpox from Old World to New, for example, were just such **virgin soil epidemics**.

Spanish explorers and the transatlantic slave trade brought smallpox, measles, flu, bubonic plague, diphtheria, typhus, cholera, scarlet fever, chickenpox, yellow fever, and whooping cough to the New World. These diseases were big contributors to the estimated 97 percent drop in the Native American population between about A.D. 1500 and 1900; now, railroads and airplanes can transport microbes even faster than sailing ships did.

Transportation isn't the only technology that created new ways for microbes to disperse. Hypodermic needles, first used in 1844, have given microbes a new express route into our bloodstream via blood transfusions, allergy injections, and illegal narcotics. This is a particularly serious problem in less developed countries, where needles are relatively rare, very expensive, and often reused by doctors and nurses.

New technology has also created new microbial habitats. Kitty litter, for example, has

Air conditioning gave bacteria that cause Legionaire's disease a new dispersal route.

given toxoplasmosis a route to spread from cats to humans. The first known major outbreak of Legionnaire's disease, caused by the bacterium *Legionella pneumophila*, was tracked to a hotel air conditioning system. The microbe was not new, but technology has given it a new aerosol dispersal route.

Global climate change will create some new health problems and worsen some old ones, like allergies. It's already changing the natural ranges and distributions of a wide variety of species, including many microbes and their vectors: Mosquitoes, ticks, and other tropical and subtropical vector organisms are being found farther north, at higher altitudes, and in greater numbers.

One of the most profound effects of agriculture is how it changes habitats, primarily through deforestation—that is, clearing land for pastures and crops—which brings humans into contact with entirely new species of pathogens. Any such disruption in an ecosystem can give some species the opportunity for rapid population growth.

Which brings us to the subject of death by chocolate: Chocolate is a dry fruit, botanically speaking, whose flowers are pollinated by tiny midges. The product we eat comes from the seeds of the *Theobroma cacao* plant. Most chocolate comes from West Africa, but a big portion of it comes from the Caribbean and from South America.

In Belém, Brazil, in the early 1960s, over 11,000 residents came down with a mysterious flulike illness. The disease turned out to be Oropouche fever, a vector-borne illness first described among the people of Trinidad and Tobago.

What caused the sudden outbreak in Belém? Land had been cleared for chocolate plantations along the then-new Bélem-Brasilia road. This clearance disturbed the habitat of the forest midge *Culicoides paraensis,* a vector for Oropouche fever. The midge found a new habitat in the discarded fruit shells from the plantations, and the microbe found virgin soil among the plantations' workers. The story of Oropouche fever demonstrates how ecosystem **disturbance** can become an evolutionary opportunity, particularly for r-selected species like microbes. ■

disturbance: Any force or factor that perturbs the normal functioning of an ecosystem.

herd immunity: A complete or partial immunity in the surviving population (the remaining "herd") after an epidemic.

naïve population: An isolated population that has not been systematically exposed to an infectious disease.

virgin soil epidemic: An epidemic in a population not previously exposed to that disease.

Suggested Reading

Despommier, *West Nile Story*.

Garrett, *The Coming Plague*.

Questions to Consider

1. In addition to those discussed in our lecture, can you think of any other ways that technology and modern lifestyles have created new opportunities for microorganisms?

2. What are some of the ways in which agriculture encourages the evolution and spread of infectious diseases or parasites?

Bambi's Revenge
Lecture 9

Human innovations from agriculture to warfare present new opportunities for the microbes that surround us. The great epidemics of tomorrow may already be lurking in some forgotten corner of Earth, waiting for an unwary victim to carry them far and wide.

Until World War II, microbes killed far more soldiers than ever died in battle. During wars, public health and sanitation programs grind to a halt; malnutrition is widespread; soldiers, prisoners, and refugees live in crowded, unsanitary conditions; and local environments suffer profound disturbance. Invading troops bring new diseases to native populations and take new diseases home with them after the war.

War, however, is not the only cause of disturbance and exposure. Suburbanization is an equal culprit. In 1975, children in Old Lyme, Connecticut, began reporting aches and pains in their bones and joints, mild fevers, general malaise, and memory problems. The syndrome became known as Lyme disease, caused by the bacterium *Borrelia burgdorferi*, carried by deer ticks of the genus *Ixodes*.

Why the sudden mysterious appearance and rapid spread of Lyme disease? Deforestation for agriculture led to an explosion in the white-tailed deer population across North America. The expansion of suburbs into cleared farmland brought large numbers of people into regular contact with deer habitats, where infected ticks were waiting in the grass.

Deforestation brought deer ticks into closer contact with humans.

33

When a new microbe comes into contact with humans, there is a danger that it will prefer human hosts to its original hosts. African relapsing fever, carried by *Borrelia duttoni*, is a disease related to Lyme disease that now occurs only in ticks and humans; it has bypassed all the intermediate hosts it used to prefer. There is a chance this could happen with the Lyme disease microbe as well.

Agriculture has also altered microbe habitats through irrigation. Fluke worms like *Clonorchis* and *Schistosoma* take advantage of irrigation farming to reach human hosts, especially in developing nations, where human waste may be used as fertilizer. *Clonorchis sinensis* infects 20 million East Asians and can cause severe jaundice and liver cancer. *Schistosoma* can cause anemia, diarrhea, brain damage, and damage to many other organs, with a fatality rate of about 25 percent.

The great epidemics of tomorrow may come from similar technology- and weather-driven changes in the ecosystem. We have already had several close calls.

Natural changes in the environment can also create new opportunities for microbes. Take, for example, the hantavirus. Of the 22 types found worldwide, 18 are found in the New World, all associated with rodent vectors. Many New World strains cause hantavirus pulmonary syndrome (HPS)—fever, muscle aches, headaches, and cough. HPS strains are extremely virulent and eventually progress to respiratory failure and death in about 50 percent of all victims.

The primary vector for the Sin Nombre hantavirus, an HPS strain identified in the American Southwest in 1993, was the deer mouse *Peromyscus*. The vector and microbe were not new to the area, but the environmental effects of El Niño fueled rapid growth of vegetation that fed the mice. Thus the mouse population exploded, bringing mice into closer contact with the nearby human population.

The great epidemics of tomorrow may come from similar technology- and weather-driven changes in the ecosystem. We have already had several close calls. A sample of virus that causes Lassa fever, a form of hemorrhagic fever that arose in Nigeria in 1969, was brought to a Yale University laboratory and infected a researcher. That one infection could have spread the disease to New England and beyond had the victim not been quickly isolated and treated.

One of the latest forms of hemorrhagic fever to emerge is Ebola, named after the Ebola River in the Congo, where it was first described in 1976. It is a **zoonosis**—a disease that can infect both animals and humans. Ebola is a savage killer, with a fatality rate between 50 and 90 percent. Its emergence may be yet another example of expanding agriculture bringing people into more frequent contact with the original host—in this case, fruit bats.

One of the 5 known types of Ebola, now called Ebola-Reston, almost escaped into the United States in October 1989 from infected monkeys at Hazleton Laboratories in Reston, Virginia. The army and the U.S Centers for Disease control had to be called in to contain the outbreak.

Perhaps the most frightening aspects of the Reston incident were that 6 lab workers tested positive for Ebola antibodies but displayed no symptoms, and 2 of those workers had no direct contact with infected monkeys, indicating that the microbe might have actually gone airborne. Luckily, Ebola-Reston turned out to be harmless to humans, but the next zoonosis may not be so benign. ■

Important Term

zoonosis: A disease that pass directly from a vertebrate animal to humans and back, with no intermediate vector such as an insect.

Suggested Reading

Harper and Meyer, *Of Mice, Men, and Microbes*.

Karlen, *Biography of a Germ*.

Preston, *The Hot Zone*.

1. How does warfare promote the spread of infectious diseases?

2. Why is the emergence of so many different diseases connected to deforestation?

The Germ of Laziness
Lecture 10

A microscopic worm may have altered the course of American history by contributing to the defeat of the Confederate army in the Civil War. The eradication of this so-called germ of laziness not only helped individuals but improved the social, political, and economic prospects of the entire American South.

Nematode worms, also called roundworms, are among the most abundant, most diverse, and least understood creatures on this planet. A typical shovel full of garden soil could hold over a million worms, and a single acre of farmland might shelter a billion. Ninety percent of the life on the ocean floor consists of nothing but different species of nematode worms.

We think of dirt as something solid, but on a microscopic scale, it's riddled with tiny irregular spaces between the fragments of minerals, dead vegetation, bits of bugs, and other natural materials. Nematodes wriggle through this complex maze of tiny irregular spaces, this **interstitial habitat**, keeping soil loose and open, letting water and air into the dirt, and easing the passage of roots.

Many nematodes are carnivorous, eating tiny creatures like algae, but about 16,000 species of nematodes are parasites. *Necator americanus*, the American hookworm, is a parasite that causes millions of people to be labeled ignorant, lazy, and

Nematodes are necessary for soil fertility, but they can cause diseases as well.

shiftless. In the early 20th century, it was dubbed "the germ of laziness" by the *New York Sun*, much to the chagrin of its discoverer, Charles Wardell Stiles.

Hookworms are extremely common and globally distributed. Roughly 10 percent of the planet's population is currently infected. Hookworm disease was known to the ancient Egyptians and was described at length by the Persian physician Avicenna in the 11th century A.D. *N. americanus* probably arrived in the New World with the slave trade. Today, it's found throughout the tropics, in the Southwest Pacific, in Africa, and throughout Asia.

Hookworm infected about 40 percent of all Southerners, primarily in poor rural areas. But this widespread infection and suffering was virtually unrecognized.

The female hookworm lays up to 30,000 eggs a day in the intestine of an infected person. The eggs are shed in feces. Young worms can live in the soil for several weeks. When a bare foot rests on the soil, the worm burrows into the skin. Once in the body, it migrates through the blood. When it arrives in the small intestine, it attaches itself to the intestinal lining, starting the cycle again.

Victims of hookworms become pale, anemic, and suffer severe digestive problems. Their muscles become weak and their abdomen may protrude. They have unusual dietary cravings for chalk paper, and dirt—a phenomenon called **pica**. Severe infections retard growth and leave the victim shrunken and malformed. Hookworm victims appear gaunt and haggard, with a sallow complexion.

The poor condition of Southern soldiers with chronic hookworm infections due to unsanitary camp conditions may have contributed to the outcome of the Civil War. The soil, climate, primitive sanitary conditions, and little to no medical care provided a nearly perfect breeding ground for hookworms in the old South. At its peak in the late 19th and early 20th century, hookworm infected about 40 percent of all Southerners, primarily in poor rural areas. But this widespread infection and suffering was virtually unrecognized.

Charles Wardell Stiles discovered *N. americanus* in Texas in 1902 while working for the U.S. Department of Agriculture. After describing this new species, he toured the South looking for hookworm; to his surprise, he found it everywhere, with infection rates ranging from 40 to 82 percent. With funding from John D. Rockefeller, he founded the Rockefeller Sanitary Commission for the Eradication of Hookworm Disease and set about eradicating the infection.

Fortunately, hookworm is easy to cure with thymol, an extract from the thyme plant. Unfortunately, it is also too easy for a patient to be reinfected. Stiles not only had to treat the victims; he had to convince whole communities to adopt lifestyle changes like shoe wearing and indoor plumbing—both expensive prospects among the rural poor at that time.

The commission's eventual, hard-fought success created a healthier Southern working class, which enabled the growth of industry in the South. School attendance and school performance also increased, as did agricultural productivity—a happy ending to a sad story.

In what may be the oddest twist of fate, hookworm infection has recently been proposed as an experimental cure for asthma. Hookworms produce immunosuppressants that could be useful in treating not only asthma but diseases such as ulcerative colitis, Crohn's disease, and multiple sclerosis. ∎

Important Terms

interstitial habitat: A habitat within and among the grains of soil in terrestrial or aquatic habitats.

pica: A dietary craving for nonfood items such as chalk and dirt; sometimes a symptom of nematode infection.

Suggested Reading

Brown, *Rockefeller Medicine Men*.

Ettling, *The Germ of Laziness*.

Wray, *Not Quite White*.

1. Was John D. Rockefeller's gift of $1 million to fund hookworm eradication primarily philanthropic, or was he making a calculated financial investment in a new industrial base?

2. If nematodes are so incredibly abundant and widespread, why have most of us never seen one?

The 1918 Flu—A Conspiracy of Silence
Lecture 11

The deadliest epidemic of all time was 1918 Flu, which killed 50–100 million people. The story of the epidemic shows us, for better or worse, how society responds to a public health crisis. By learning how and why we were so vulnerable, we may be better equipped to save ourselves when the next global pandemic strikes.

The Spanish influenza epidemic of 1918 was one of the great watershed events in the history of the world. Flu was nothing new in 1918. The first global flu pandemic occurred in 1580, starting in Asia and sweeping across Europe. Between 1700 and 1900 there were at least 16 major flu epidemics. The last major pandemic was in 1889–1890, the first of what were later called the Asian flus.

Nobody knows exactly where the 1918 Flu began, but Dr. Loring Miner of Haskell County, Kansas, reported dozens of patients stricken by an unusually virulent form of the flu between January and mid-March of 1918. There it might have ended in such an isolated community, but America was at war, and in wartime, people move between populations more often and in greater numbers.

Twenty-four of the 36 largest U.S. army camps reported an outbreak of flu in the spring of 1918, along with 30 of the country's 50 largest cities. Meanwhile, over 1.5 million American soldiers were being sent to Europe, the largest troop movement in the history of the world, and many of them were unknowingly incubating the disease.

The flu soon spread to French and British troops, and Allied soldiers took it home to civilians while on leave. The virus spread rapidly to Germany, Russia, China, India, southeast Asia, and Spain, becoming a true global pandemic. It was dubbed the Spanish Flu only because the press started to take notice as it hit Spain.

Something happened aboard the troopships or in the foul and crowded trenches that turned a mild flu into a savage killer. It is possible that a new and entirely different strain of flu from the Kansas virus had emerged; a genetic **mutation** may have altered the original strain; or 2 different viruses may have fused to create a new strain.

Within 10 hours of infection, that cell can release 100,000 to 1 million or more new flu viruses.

Viruses generally consist of a core of RNA or DNA surrounded by a membrane or capsule. Unlike cells, viruses cannot replicate by themselves; they take over the protein factory of a living cell and reprogram it to make copies of the virus. Influenza is an **RNA virus** whose membrane is covered 2 kinds of **antigen** spikes: H spikes and N spikes. (Different flu strains are named for their spike configurations, like H5N1.) The H spikes, made of hemagglutinin, cause red blood cells to clump, or agglutinate. The N spikes are neuraminidase, an **enzyme**.

Every organism has a different pattern of antigens on the surface of its cells. The immune system recognizes these antigens as cellular ID tags and uses them to separate self from nonself. Small changes in antigen structure, called **antigenic drift**, create variant strains. Larger changes, called **antigenic shifts**, create subtypes. Antigenic shifts are responsible for major new outbreaks of flu.

The flu virus uses its H spikes like grappling hooks to attach itself to the outside of a cell. The cell absorbs the virus through phagocytosis, wrapping the virus in a bubble of cell membrane. Once inside the cell, the virus sheds its envelope and releases its RNA genes, which hijack the cellular protein. Within 10 hours of infection, that cell can release 100,000 to 1 million or more new flu viruses. Then new viruses' N spikes chemically slice through the cell membrane and go in to infect new cells.

In the case of the 1918 Flu, the fact that survivors of the first mild wave had some immunity to later waves tells us that the second wave wasn't an entirely new strain but an altered form of the first virus with different surface antigens. An RNA virus, like the flu, has **hypermutability**—a mutation rate thousands and thousands of times higher than a DNA virus.

This altered strain the flu struck with amazing intensity. Symptoms were so severe that doctors often misdiagnosed the flu as malaria or dengue fever. The immune system reaction was so strong that it often created a disastrous feedback loop called a **cytokine storm**, destroying the lungs' ability to exchange gas. Some survivors were left with permanent nerve damage and even psychosis.

Casualty figures for the fall of 1918 show the brutal power of the virus: nearly 23,000 flu deaths in military hospitals, and we'll never know how many thousands or tens of thousands more in foxholes and trenches on the front. But the battle with the 1918 Flu did not end on the battlefields of Europe, as we will soon see. ∎

Important Terms

antigen: A fragment of a cell or protein that can be detected by the immune system; also, a molecule or cell with an epitope in its structure.

antigenic drift: A significant alteration in the structure of the surface proteins of a virus, effectively disguising it from the immune system. Usually refers to influenza, especially the structure of H spikes and N spikes.

antigenic shift: A dramatic alteration in the structure of the surface proteins of a virus sufficient to trigger an epidemic.

cytokine storm: A cascade reaction of defensive proteins that can prove fatal—the immune system's equivalent of a thermonuclear attack.

enzyme: A protein that can act as a chemical catalyst, mediating a reaction without being changed by it. Enzymes control the rate, direction, synthesis, and degradation of many biochemical reactions in the body. Most of what our genes actually code for are different kinds of enzymes.

hypermutability: The tendency of certain organisms, such as the influenza virus, to mutate at a relatively high rate.

mutation: A random alteration of genetic information that can occur in RNA or DNA.

RNA virus: A virus whose genetic material consists solely of RNA (not DNA). Because such viruses lack the proofreading mechanism that governs the reproduction of DNA, they mutate at a very high rate.

Suggested Reading

Crosby, *America's Forgotten Pandemic*.

Pettit and Bailie, *A Cruel Wind*.

Barry, *The Great Influenza*.

Questions to Consider

1. Because influenza is an RNA virus, it lacks the proofreading mechanism that a DNA virus would have, and its control over replication and reverse transcription is rather messy. Why does this sloppiness turn out to be a big advantage for the virus?

2. What makes a virus fundamentally different from a bacterium when it comes time to reproduce?

The 1918 Flu—The Philadelphia Story
Lecture 12

The city of Philadelphia is a case study of how American cities responded to the 1918 Flu pandemic, but the flu also hit isolated native populations especially hard. Everyone on Earth at one time was probably exposed to the virus; in the end, the pandemic only subsided because it had no new hosts within the human population.

Most authorities think that the American flu mutated into a killer in its new European population. The new strain likely re-entered the United States on August 12, 1918, via the Norwegian passenger ship the *Bergensfjord*, which entered New York harbor with 200 sick passengers who disembarked and scattered into the New York City population. Over half a million Americans would die in their wake.

One of the reasons the flu was so terrifying at that time was that no one had any real idea of what had caused it. After the 1889–1890 flu pandemic, Dr. Richard Pfeiffer had isolated a bacterium now known as Pfeiffer's bacillus. It's a very dangerous microbe but not, as it turned out, the cause of the 1918 Flu.

There was also little to be done for the sick. Medical treatment consisted mostly in comforting and isolating the patient if possible—in other words, basic nursing. Public health responses included fumigation, urging people to wear gauze masks, campaigns against spitting and sneezing, warnings about public gatherings, and a general prescription for rest and fresh air. Folk cures abounded; snake oil salesmen were everywhere.

Philadelphia was typical of big cities ravaged by the flu. Overcrowding, inadequate social services, and squalid living conditions amongst the poor made the city the perfect breeding ground for infection. Influenza entered the city in mid-September 1918 via the navy yard. On September 27, some 200 flu cases had been reported, 123 of them among civilians. Nonetheless, the city fathers refused to cancel the Liberty Loan Parade, designed to sell war bonds, scheduled for the next day.

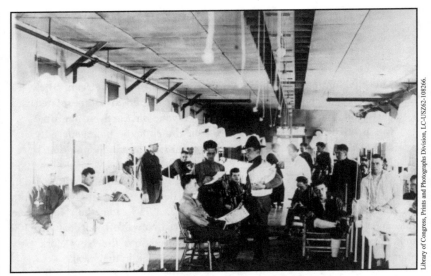

An infirmary at Camp Devens, Massachusetts, full of soldiers infected with the 1918 Flu. At its peak, the Devens outbreak claimed 100 lives per day.

The flu's **incubation period** is typically 24–48 hours. By September 30, several hundred people had fallen ill. Twelve emergency hospitals would eventually open to receive the growing number of the sick and dying. The call went out for retired doctors to come back to work; all 5 Philadelphia medical schools closed and sent their third and fourth year students to help.

On October 3, the government ordered all schools, churches, and theaters to close and banned all public gatherings. Most grocers were closed and few stores of any kind were open. Absentee rates ran from 20 to 40 percent for those businesses and factories still functioning. As the epidemic peaked during the week of October 16, 4597 people died—759 of them on October 10 alone.

The city resorted to burying the poor in mass graves. Citizens were given wooden boxes and instructed to leave their dead on the front porch. Some bodies were heaped into wagons, reminiscent of scenes from the Black Death. People often had to live with dead bodies in their homes for several days. Every social agency in the city chipped in to help as best they could, without regard to race, creed, or color.

By October 18, the worst was over and emergency hospitals began to close. Churches reopened on Sunday, October 27, and schools reopened the next day. On October 30, bars and theaters reopened.

A third and final wave followed in late 1918 and ran through early 1919. The virus seems to have gradually mutated into a weaker strain at this point because the third wave was short and sharp but relatively mild.

Estimates of American dead run to 675,000 out of a population of 105 million. Britain lost 228,000. The best global estimate is 50–100 million dead out of 1.8 billion.

Estimates of American dead run to 675,000 out of a population of 105 million. Britain lost 228,000. The best global estimate is 50–100 million dead out of 1.8 billion.

Naïve native populations were especially hard hit because they lacked previous exposure and immunity. American Samoa survived without a single victim because of its early quarantine, and Australia had the lowest global death rate because of its relative isolation. But, for example, in the Fiji Islands, 14 percent of the population died in 16 days. In Alaska, many Inuit villages sustained an 85 percent casualty rate or higher. Over 20 million people are thought to have died in India alone.

Those who survived the 1918 Flu developed immunity to it and **resistance** to similar strains. Thus in the end, the virus had no place left to go; it couldn't maintain itself in the human population. Fortunately for the flu virus (and unfortunately for us), it doesn't need humanity to sustain itself. Birds are its primary host, and as long as bird populations are healthy, the flu will always find a home. ■

Important Terms

incubation period: Period of time between infection and the first symptoms of an infection. Sometimes called the latency period, although that term usually refers to the time between infection and becoming infectious to others.

resistance: A physiological trait that helps prevent infection by pathogens. Although often used as synonym for immunity, resistance is a physical feature that can be directly inherited (like lacking a certain protein on the cell wall that a virus could use to enter the cell), whereas immunity is a cellular memory of a disease in the form of stored antibodies.

Suggested Reading

Duncan, *Hunting the 1918 Flu*.

Kolata, *Flu*.

Questions to Consider

1. What does the response of Philadelphia's citizens to the flu epidemic tell us about how people in general behave in a medical crisis?

2. Why did a greater proportion of native tribes in isolated areas die from the 1918 Flu versus urban populations?

The 1918 Flu—The Search for the Virus
Lecture 13

In 1918, the flu was a horror story; today, it is a detective story, as scientists search for an intact virus. This is no mere intellectual exercise; in the wrong hands, the virus could make a formidable weapon; if we can decode its genes, we might find a way to fight it or any similar strain.

One surprising, lingering effect of the 1918 Flu was how it helped set the stage for World War II. President Woodrow Wilson began the treaty negotiations with a harsh stance against the aggressors. But after his struggle with the flu in April 1919, those close to Wilson reported a dramatic personality change. Soon, Wilson made every concession he had previously refused.

Historians speculate that Wilson suffered a mild stroke during the talks, but the 1918 Flu left many of its victims with permanent mental and neurological damage. Whatever the case, the Treaty of Versailles did not solve the problems of World War I and helped to create the conditions that led to World War II.

What if the 1918 Flu or a similar strain were to return today? Would we be prepared to fight it? In many ways, we are more vulnerable than ever. The 1918 Flu spread rapidly by rail and ocean liner; modern highways and global airlines would disperse such a killer even more effectively. Our increasingly interconnected global trade system leaves each nation less self-reliant, so a global pandemic might trigger a cascade of economic collapse, leading to shortages of critical items, even food.

Being more vulnerable means we have to be better prepared, starting with a better understanding of what made this strain so dangerous. The U.S. Army preserved many lung tissue samples from dead soldiers. Jeffery Taubenberger and Ann Reid of the Armed Forces Institute of Pathology have begun trying to isolate the virus from such a sample. Pathologist Johan Hultin found samples in a mass grave at Brevig Mission, Alaska, in 1997 in a victim he dubbed "Lucy," from which Taubenberger was able to sequence several viral genes.

Several mysteries surrounding the 1918 Flu remain unsolved. Normally, the flu is most deadly to those with the weakest immune systems—the young, the old, and the already ill. Some doctors think the massive lung damage seen in young victims of the 1918 Flu was partly due to a deadly cytokine storm. On the other hand, young adults in 1918 may have had especially high levels of tuberculosis, leaving their damaged lungs ripe for invasion by influenza.

A multi-billion dollar international effort is currently underway to study H5N1 and prepare for a possible future outbreak.

Flu is driven by herd immunity to undergo major antigenic shifts every 2 or 3 years. But the 3 waves of the 1918 Flu were very close together; in a few places, it's hard to say when one ended and the next began. That tight spacing lends some support to the argument that that second wave was a hybrid virus or a mutant strain, sufficiently different to overcome the partial immunity of survivors of the first wave. Cycles of the 1918 Flu were so out of step that many scientists have come to doubt the validity of the whole idea of **epidemiologic cycles**, at least where the flu is concerned. Or perhaps we are missing a much larger pattern.

Flu is a rather unusual microbe in that new subtypes of flu tend to drive all old subtypes into extinction; only one subtype and one variant tends to exist in humans at a time. This may be because each new subtype provokes a general partial immunity to flu viruses. So when older strains cycle back into fresh populations, the door may be already closed.

The molecular evidence suggests that the 1918 Flu was H1N1, a novel strain of bird flu which later spread to swine and humans. The 1976 swine flu was an H1N1 variant, which is why it caused an international panic, and a record 40 million people got a flu shot that year. If nothing else, that 1976 swine flu scare prepared us for another epidemiological nightmare: A modern outbreak or a terrorist attack with weaponized flu would require a similar scheme of mass inoculation.

In 1997, an explosive outbreak of avian flu struck in Hong Kong. This was a new strain called H5N1. Six out of every 18 infected people died. That could have been the beginning of a serious new pandemic, but rapid quarantine and the destruction of every single chicken in Hong Kong stopped it in its tracks. H5N1 is currently the most dangerous type of flu in circulation. A multi-billion dollar international effort is currently underway to study H5N1 and prepare for a possible future outbreak.

The 2009 Swine Flu virus was an H1N1 subtype, like the 1918 Flu, which is one reason why doctors overreacted so strongly to that outbreak. Initial analysis of the 2009 swine flu pandemic indicated a higher mortality rate for young adults, just like the 1918 Flu, and once again caused by extreme cytokine storms. If the 1918 Flu or a similar strain does return, we may be prepared for it this time. An experimental **DNA vaccine** developed by the U.S. National Institutes of Health has been found to be effective against a live reconstructed 1918 virus. ■

Important Terms

DNA vaccine: Plasmids that code for a critical protein in the life cycle of a particular microbe.

epidemiologic cycle: The demographic pattern of infection or mortality over time in a given population.

Suggested Reading

Blakely, *Mass Mediated Disease.*

Jones, *Influenza 1918.*

1. Why doesn't our annual flu shot always work?

2. In what way are we more vulnerable during a major flu epidemic, as individuals and as a society, than our parents' generation?

Immunity—Self versus Nonself
Lecture 14

You might be starting to wonder why humans aren't all sick all of the time. For that, you can thank your immune system, your first line of defense against infection. This extremely complex system saves our lives every day, but it can also turn on us, sometimes with fatal consequences.

There are thousands and thousands of tiny organisms whose only goal in life is to survive and reproduce in or on you. All kinds of creatures can live in the diverse habitats that exist inside our cells, and they've evolved many strategies for exploiting the human body. We need a complex immune system to deal with that endless diversity.

The immune system has evolved to master the difficult art of telling the difference between self and nonself. That's not as easy as you might think. It must recognize and kill invaders without harming the host. In other words, it must learn self-tolerance.

Our immune system consists of many specialized cells. One of the most important defensive cells is the leukocyte, or white blood cell. Leukocytes actually can be found not just in the blood but all throughout the body. There are many different types with many different functions, but the 3 main types are **phagocytes**, or eating cells; **cytotoxic cells**, or killing cells; and **inflammatory cells**, which are responsible for local inflammation.

Phagocytes literally wrap themselves around microbes and pinch off a little part of their outer membrane to enclose the microbe in a tiny little sphere called a vesicle or a vacuole. Once inside, lysosomes, organelles that hold digestive enzymes, are used to kill and digest the microbes. That simple act of good cells killing bad cells is part of what we call cellular immunity.

Russian zoologist Élie Metchnikoff won the Nobel Prize in 1908 for discovering cellular immunity. His focus was comparative embryology, but while studying the larvae of starfish, he became curious about groups of amoeba-like cells he saw moving through the starfish larvae. He thought these eating cells formed a primal digestive system in the early evolution of animal body plans. He also reasoned that these cells might be part of the larvae's defense system.

One of phagocytes' many functions is to devour all the dead cells and the debris at the site of wounds or infections. Recent studies suggest they also have a much broader role in maintaining our tissues, like ensuring the structural integrity of vascular tissue.

Phagocytes, along with cytotoxic cells and inflammatory cells, are part of what we call **innate immunity**. But the white cells involved in innate immunity are very unusual in one key respect: They're the only cells in our body that aren't associated with a specific tissue or organ.

Defensive cells "recognize" invaders the way a lock "recognizes" its key. Phagocytes are covered in surface receptors; if they encounter a microbe with surface molecules that fit one of their receptors, they can latch on to it.

Cytotoxic cells are our second line of defense. Cytotoxic cells don't poison microbes, as the name implies; they stab them to death. **Natural killer (NK) cells** are cytotoxic cells unique to vertebrates. NK cells don't kill microbes directly but rather kill the cells that those microbes have invaded. They specialize in tumor cells or cells that have been infected by a virus. They release a protein called perforin that perforates the cell walls of the infected cells, through which the NK cells send molecules that cause the infected cell to commit suicide, taking any invading microbes along with it. NK cells also release cytokines.

NK cells look for cells that lack a cellular ID card called the **major histocompatibility complex (MHC)**. MHC molecules haul bits and pieces of the cell's proteins to the surface of the cell where they are visible to any passing NK cell. If a virus is at work, pieces of viral proteins will be hauled to the surface as well, where they will be spotted by passing killer cells.

The inflammatory cells, our third line of defense, create an inflammatory response that is local and nonspecific. The chemicals that cause local swelling attract swarms of phagocytes, cytotoxic cells, and defensive proteins called **antibodies**. The most important inflammatory cells are **mast cells** and basophils They respond to injury or attack by releasing chemicals like histamine that cause our capillaries to dilate, making them more permeable, which allows the phagocytes to pass through.

In addition to defensive cells, our bodies have evolved many different proteins that can attack microbes. Interferon, for example, attacks viruses. The complement system, a more primitive protein-based defense system, is a group of about 25 proteins that build up on the surface of a microbe. They may

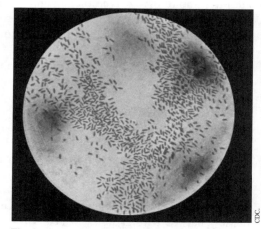

The immune system identifies bacteria, like these *Haemophilus influenzae*, by their cell-surface molecules.

destroy the microbe themselves or may release chemicals to attract other immune cells. They also **opsonize** invading cells, coating them with proteins that help phagocytes bind to them.

Higher animals have **adaptive immunity** as well as innate immunity. Their immune systems aren't limited to recognizing a small number of basic patterns. Rather than looking for patterns of sugar molecules like those found on a bacterial cell wall, they look for pattern differences in proteins—specifically, for groups of amino acids called **epitopes**, unique molecules found on the surface of antigens. The adaptive immune system has to make a different type of antigen receptor to match each different epitope—potentially over 100 million different epitopes. ■

adaptive immunity: A type of immunity evolved by higher animals that doesn't look for general patterns of shared structure but rather for minute differences in molecules shared by hosts and microbes.

antibody: A protein that can attach to a corresponding epitope and flag a cell or molecule for destruction by the immune system.

cytotoxic cell: A type of defensive cell common to all animals that effectively stabs foreign cells to death by punching holes through their cell walls.

epitope: A fragment of protein from a cell or molecule that can be detected by the immune system.

inflammatory cell: A cell involved in the inflammatory response that is densely packed with granules loaded with potent chemical mediators like histamine.

innate immunity: A primitive type of immune system common to a wide variety of animals that gives certain cells the ability to identify foreign cells by recognizing patterns of sugar molecules in their cell walls. Phaogcytes, cytotoxic cells, and inflammatory cells are components of innate immunity.

major histocompatability complex (MHC): A receptor site on the outside of every vertebrate cell that can hold onto an epitope or antigen so that immune system cells can recognize it.

mast cell: An inflammatory cell that releases the cytokine histamine.

natural killer cell (NK cell): A cytotoxic cell that seeks out and destroys cells invaded by microbes; NK cells specialize in attacking cancerous cells or cells invaded by a virus.

opsonization: Part of the complement system; a process through which an invading cell is coated with proteins that help phagocytes bind to them.

phagocyte: An amoeboid "eating cell" found in all types of animals that can engulf and consume other microbes.

Suggested Reading

Clark, *In Defense of Self.*

Playfair, *Living with Germs.*

Questions to Consider

1. I have type O blood and my friend has type AB. When it comes to blood transfusion, why am I the universal donor, and why is he the universal recipient?

2. What is it about larger, more complex animal bodies that made the adaptive immune system necessary?

Adaptive Immunity to the Rescue
Lecture 15

Defensive cells have to master the fine art of recognizing epitopes to fight off foreign invaders. Once an epitope is recognized, this sets off a virtual army of different cells in a coordinated response that destroys the microbe and stores the memory of the attack for use in the future.

Our cells can potentially detect over 100 million different kinds of epitopes thanks to our **lymphocytes**, which are types of leukocytes. There are 3 basic types of lymphocytes: **NKT cells**, **T cells**, and **B cells**. NKT, or natural killer T cells, act just like NK cells but also act as messengers, releasing cytokines to stimulate the immune response.

Lymphocytes, among other cell types, are made by bone marrow stem cells. Each stem cell has several hundred genes that code for antigen receptor shapes. Every new lymphocyte gets a starter kit, a random set of 5 or 6 of these receptor genes, just enough to put together one unique antigen receptor. A few hundred genes, parceled out this way can easily make more than 100 million different antigen receptors. But this clever system has a hidden cost: Among those millions of random variations will be a handful that match our own antigens—what we would call a "self-reactive" epitope.

Any unique epitope could be recognized by any of several different kinds of lymphocytes, a process called presentation. But there are so many different kinds of lymphocytes, the body can't keep more than a few of each type around at any one time. When an invader is recognized, the matching lymphocyte has to copy itself to create an army, a process called activation. This phase of the infection is called the primary immune response.

To thwart future attacks from that same microbe, the adaptive immune system makes **memory cells** that are matched to that particular microbe. These memory cells can live for several years, and if the invader returns, we can build up a new population of cloned soldiers so quickly that we might not even have any symptoms of infection at all. We are now said to be immune to that disease. This "return engagement" phase is called the secondary immune response.

B cells and T cells are especially important in this process. Both are made in bone marrow; B cells mature in the marrow, while T cells migrate and mature in the thymus gland. The B cells are the deputies; they check cellular IDs for known villains and they mark them with antibodies. Antibodies can directly neutralize some toxins made by microbes and can prevent some microbes from binding to our cells. But their most important function is to pin a flag on invading microbes to call out the posse—the T cells, which release a wide array of chemicals that marshal the attack on an invading microbe.

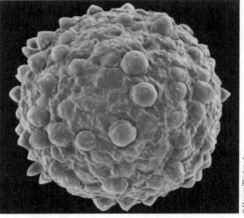

Lymphocytes act as killer cells, destroying microbes directly, and as messengers to other cells, stimulating the immune response.

At any given moment there are roughly 900 billion lymphocytes moving through your body. Most of the time, they are concentrated in the lymph nodes. When needed, a network of capillaries transports them through the lymphatic fluid throughout the body. When you have a swollen lymph node, it's a sure sign that the body is fighting off an infection.

The immune system uses messenger cells called **antigen-presenting cells (APCs)**—including **macrophages**, B cells, and **dendritic cells**—to signal to T cells that an infection has begun. APCs run the invading microbe's epitope up their own molecular flagpole, the MHC—specifically MHC class II. APCs then approach the nearest lymph node and present the foreign antigen to the T cells, hoping to find one whose antigen receptor fits. If it finds a match, the T cell activates. Different groups of APCs tend to patrol each particular part of the body. T cells can recognize each group and know where to find the infection.

There are 2 kinds of T cells: **helper T cells (T_H cells)** and **killer T cells (T_C cells)**. APCs release the cytokine interleukin-1, which activates the T_H cell and stimulates the hypothalamus to raise body temperatures, causing a fever. Fever stimulates the macrophages to start eating bacteria and causes the liver and the spleen to begin iron withholding. The T_H cell releases interleukin-2, which triggers the activation of T_C cells and B cells.

At any given moment there are roughly 900 billion lymphocytes moving through your body.

The activated T_C cell clones itself and goes off to seek the enemy. The B cells split into 2 lines: plasma cells and memory cells. The plasma cells make antibodies, and the memory cells hold onto the proper receptor site in case the invader ever returns. The point when antibodies appear in the bloodstream is called the **humoral response**.

The terms "immunity" and "resistance" are often used interchangeably, but they don't quite mean the same thing. Resistance comes from a structural change in a cell or in a molecule—changes that are coded for in our genes and can therefore be inherited. Immunity is learned resistance—something we acquire only by encountering a new disease. It does not change our genes, and we cannot inherit it or pass it on. ■

Important Terms

antigen-presenting cell (APC): Immune system cells that act as messengers by carrying antigens on their major histocompatability complex to the corresponding T cells for activation. APCs include macrophages, B cells, and dendritic cells.

B cell: A type of lymphocyte whose function is to produce antibodies for specific antigens and to form memory cells to guard against any future encounters with that same antigen.

dendritic cell: A type of lymphocyte in mammals that functions as an antigen-presenting cell, helping to bridge the gap between the innate and adaptive immune systems.

helper T cell (a.k.a. T_H **or CD4+ cells**): A critical immune system T cell that, when activated, coordinates a wide range of immune processes through the secretion of messenger molecules called cytokines.

humoral response: Part of the primary immune response; the activation of B cells by helper T cells to make antibodies (plasma cells) and memory cells.

killer T cells (T_C or CD8+ cells): Cytotoxic T cells that are especially good at killing cells that are cancerous or have been infected with a virus. *See* **cytotoxic cell** and **helper T cell**.

lymphocytes: Cells involved in adaptive immunity.

macrophage: An immune cell common to most animals that "eats" pathogens. Macrophages can travel almost anywhere in the body, devour pathogens, and carry them to the lymph nodes to trigger an immune response.

memory cell: An activated B cell that is relatively long-lived and can be rapidly cloned if the same antigen or invader returns.

natural killer T cell (NKT cell): A cell that acts like a regular natural killer cell but can also mediate adaptive immune responses by releasing messenger chemicals called cytokines.

T cell: A lymphocyte that plays many key roles in the immune system and has a receptor on its cell surface that lets it recognize antigens bound to the major histocompatability complex. Types include cytotoxic T cells, helper T cells, and natural killer T cells.

Mak and Saunders, *Primer to the Immune Response.*

Sompayrac, *How the Immune System Works.*

Questions to Consider

1. How can a finite number of animal genes make a sufficiently large number of proteins to match up with millions of possible microbial epitopes?

2. Why do we often get sick for a day or two when we catch a disease we're supposed to be immune to?

AIDS—The Quiet Killer
Lecture 16

AIDS may be the most virulent disease in human history. Caused by a retrovirus—a type of virus that alters its host's DNA—the disease cripples the immune system by destroying T_H cells, making every cell in the host's body a safe haven for the virus.

No one has ever truly survived infection with HIV, the virus that causes acquired immunodeficiency syndrome (AIDS) in humans. Once symptoms emerge, the fatality rate is 100 percent. There is no cure; the most we can do is slow it down. Without treatment, victims have about 11 years to live from the time of infection.

HIV relies on the fluid route for transmission, namely blood and semen. Microbes that travel in the blood often rely on insect vectors like mosquitoes or their technological counterpart, the hypodermic needle. But the trifecta for the fluid route is sex; saliva, semen, and sometimes blood are all flowing. Throw in intimate bodily contact, and you have the ideal mode for dispersal. Unsurprisingly, many of the deadliest diseases are sexually transmitted.

HIV produces no killer toxins, no violent symptoms. Instead, it cripples the immune system by striking at its most vulnerable part—the T_H cells that orchestrate the adaptive immune response. Once the virus kills enough T_H cells, the immune system can no longer coordinate an attack. AIDS victims don't die from AIDS; they die from cancer or a secondary infection.

Because an AIDS victim's body can no longer recognize a cancerous cell, any cancerous growth can be fatal. More AIDS victims die of cancer than from any other cause; 30–40 percent of AIDS victims will develop a malignant tumor. In fact, AIDS was first discovered from a cluster of Kaposi's sarcoma cases in the gay community of San Francisco in 1981.

Like so many of our worst diseases, AIDS came out of the jungle, specifically from increased human contact with other primates. Recent genetic analysis puts the virus's origin in West Africa sometime between 1930 and 1950 during a period of deforestation. As rural populations expanded, they became increasingly reliant on "bush meat" and were more likely to keep monkeys as pets.

One of the reasons that AIDS is so deadly is that it's so new. A scant 50 years have passed since the first cases appeared—not much time for humans to evolve defenses, nor for AIDS to coevolve to a less virulent strain.

Viruses usually consist of strands of **RNA** or **DNA** that are wrapped in a protein coat called a capsid. Every kind of virus is coded to attach to a particular type of cell, so they can target specific tissues and organs. A virus attacks by attaching to the outside of the cell, injecting its genetic code into the cell, taking over the cell's machinery, and using the cell to make more viruses.

The ultimate origin of viruses is a complete mystery, though there are 3 main hypotheses: the cellular origin, or vagrancy, hypothesis, which claims viruses are rogue bits of genetic material escaped from an intact cell; the coevolution hypothesis, which suggests viruses coevolved with cells; and the degeneracy, or regressive, hypothesis, which claims viruses are degenerate cells.

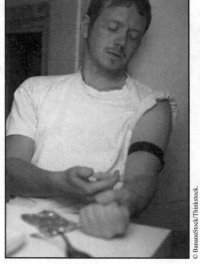

The hypodermic needle is the high-tech counterpart to the mosquito, acting as a vector for blood-borne viruses like HIV.

Viruses are strange little creatures to begin with, but HIV is strange, even for a virus. HIV is a **retrovirus**. Its core is a strip of RNA, and it uses an enzyme called **reverse transcriptase (RT)** to stitch its RNA into the host cell's DNA. In this way, it not only forces the host cell to make copies of itself; when the host cell reproduces, it passes that viral RNA on to all of its daughter cells. Even if the immune system kills every single active virus in the body, the instructions for making more will live on.

DNA contains the instructions our cells use to make proteins. RT reads the cell's DNA and maps it onto a strand of **messenger RNA (mRNA)**. This strand is a set of instructions for building a protein from amino acids. The mRNA travels to the cytoplasm, like a foreman bringing plans to the factory floor, where **ribosomal RNA (rRNA)** will read them and transfer RNA (tRNA) will use them to assemble a protein.

The ultimate origin of viruses is a complete mystery.

DNA is a chain of molecules called **nucleotides**, of which there are 4 types. A group of 3 nucleotides, called a **codon**, is used to code for each of the 20 amino acids used in making proteins. The amino acids used and the order in which they are assembled determine the final shape of the protein and thus its chemical properties. By changing the amino acid sequence, you change the protein's ability to interact with other chemicals. So in essence, retroviruses like HIV change the codons of the host's DNA, getting the cell to build the proteins needed to make a new virus—an elegant act of biological piracy. ■

Important Terms

codon: A series of 3 genetic nucleotides that code for a particular amino acid. The sequence of codons determines the proper sequence of amino acids needed to assemble a particular protein.

DNA: Two strands of complementary nucleotides attached to a molecular backbone of sugar and phosphate molecules. The sequence of nucleotides codes for the synthesis of proteins.

messenger RNA (mRNA): A form of RNA used in the synthesis of proteins that is assembled by matching complementary nucleotides (A/T, C/G) to replicate the sequence of nucleotides on a strand of DNA.

nucleotide: A biomolecule whose many important functions include carrying the genetic code. The 4 nucleotides used in DNA are adenine, guanine, cytosine, and thymine (abbreviated A, G, C, and T). RNA substitutes uracil (U) for thymine (T).

retrovirus: A virus that uses an enzyme called reverse transcriptase to convert its RNA into DNA, which is then incorporated into the host's DNA.

reverse transcriptase (RT): An enzyme used to turn viral RNA into DNA, which is then stitched into a host's DNA. This is the reverse of the normal process of transcription, in which the genetic message contained in a strand of DNA is copied or transcribed onto a strand of messenger RNA. The enzyme is used by viruses like HIV and feline leukemia virus.

ribosomal RNA (rRNA): A type of RNA that reads a strip of messenger RNA to allow transfer RNA to identify and fetch the next amino acid coded for. This in turn allows a ribosome to create a chain from the amino acids supplied by transfer RNA that will subsequently roll up into a functional protein.

RNA: A single strand of nucleotides attached to a molecular backbone of sugar and phosphate molecules. The nucleotides code for synthesis of a particular protein.

transfer RNA (tRNA): A form of RNA that to transfers amino acids from the cytoplasm to the ribosomes to be added to a chain of amino acids that will form a protein. It has a binding site on one end that matches up with a codon on messenger RNA and a binding site for the corresponding amino acid at the other.

Suggested Reading

Davis, *Defending the Body*.

Shilts, *And the Band Played On*.

1. AIDS may be the ultimate killer, yet no one has ever actually died from it. How can this be true?

2. Based on what we've learned about how humans acquire animal diseases, how would the rapid growth of biomedical research during the 1940s and 1950s have increased the odds of the emergence of a disease like AIDS?

The Deadly Strategy of AIDS
Lecture 17

By attacking the immune system, AIDS gets a double bonus. The HIV virus itself is protected, and other invading microbes stimulate T_H cell production, giving the virus more cells to attack. At the moment, there is little hope for a vaccine against HIV or a cure for AIDS; we need to focus on prevention.

As evolutionary strategies go, HIV's is a clear winner—and an ironic one. Macrophages carry fragments of the virus to our lymph nodes and present them to the T_H cells, leading them to their doom. Infected macrophages can live for years, carrying the virus to every system in the body. The more our bodies try to fight HIV, the sicker we get.

This systematic destruction of T_H cells cripples the victim's immune system. HIV can destroy 1 to 2 billion T_H cells every day—roughly 30 percent of the body's supply. Even a trivial infection could become fatal because there is no longer any way to fight back.

As if this weren't bad enough, opportunistic microbes have coevolved to take advantage of HIV's assault on the immune system. There is a real danger that these strains might spread to the general population. But the true nightmare scenario is HIV becoming airborne. Since HIV can mutate up to 1 million times faster than a standard DNA virus, anything is possible. There is a long latency between HIV infection and the appearance of AIDS symptoms—sometimes as long as a decade—so there's plenty of time for the virus to mutate within an individual. The more people infected with HIV, the greater the odds of an aerosol mutation become.

That said, even in the worst-case scenario, not everyone on Earth would die. A small handful of individuals can carry the HIV virus but aren't infected by it—they never develop AIDS. These individuals have a mutation that left their cells with a deformed or missing fusin coreceptor, so HIV can't get a grip on the surface of their cells to get inside. A handful of HIV-positive individuals are **long-term nonprogressors**—people with no symptoms 10 or more years after infection. These individuals are still losing T_H cells, though at a much slower pace.

The AIDS pandemic is increasing at an astounding rate. Over 33 million people worldwide are infected, with over 25 million deaths so far. There are about 1.5 million AIDS victims in North America, 2.25 million in South America, and 22.4 million in sub-Saharan Africa. Worldwide, there were 7400 new cases of AIDS every day in 2008; 1200 of those new cases were in children under the age of 15. Over 2 million children worldwide are currently living with AIDS. Nearly half of the newly diagnosed cases in 2008 were in women—so much for the "gay plague."

A small handful of individuals can carry the HIV virus but aren't infected by it—they never develop AIDS.

One of the reasons AIDS is raging through Africa today is that HIV is riding on the coattails of malaria, which stimulates T_H cell production. Another reason that the virus is flourishing in Asia and in Africa is social unrest. In the wake of war, anarchy, famine, and civil strife, social fabrics unravel. Casual sex with multiple partners becomes much more common, as does sharing of hypodermic needles, both of which rapidly spread the virus.

We fight AIDS with a wide variety of drugs. The current best drug is azidothymidine (AZT), which slows viral reproduction but doesn't kill the virus. The gold standard of AIDS therapy today is highly active antiretroviral therapy (HAART), a drug that combines a reverse transcriptase inhibitor with a protease inhibitor. However, HAART costs approximately $10,000 per year and is out of reach for most of the world's victims. The newest drugs are **fusion inhibitors**, which bind to HIV's fusion proteins and stop the virus from attaching itself to cell surfaces. But fusion inhibitors have to be injected twice a day and cost around $25,000 a year per patient.

Why don't we have an AIDS vaccine? Vaccines work by challenging the immune system with a small dose of fragmented or dead microbe. Because HIV only needs one active virus to get started, nobody wants to take a chance, even with a dead virus vaccine, because one live virus could slip through. Attempts to make HIV vaccines based on viral fragments, or epitopes, have so far been unsuccessful. Scientists are researching the use of a DNA vaccine to enhance the ability of T_C cells to kill HIV. Others are looking at some newly discovered antibodies from AIDS victims that seem effective against 90 percent of all known HIV strains and variants.

Our best hope to stem the AIDS pandemic is to change human behavior. The virulence of AIDS changes with changes in the frequency of sexual contact. In a population with high monogamy and low promiscuity rates, a sexually transmitted disease's best strategy is to mutate into a strain that keeps the host alive as long as possible to wait out a new contact. A less virulent strain—HIV-2—is already circulating in West Africa. Reducing the frequency of unprotected sexual contacts should help nudge AIDS toward more benign strains. Distributing free condoms and free sterile needles would go a long way toward slowing down the AIDS pandemic. ∎

Important Terms

fusion inhibitor: A type of AIDS drug that prevents HIV from fusing with the surface of a cell to inject its contents.

long-term nonprogressor: An HIV-positive individual who has avoided developing the symptoms of AIDS for 10 years or more.

Suggested Reading

Barnett and Whiteside, *AIDS in the Twenty-First Century*.

Epstein, *The Invisible Cure*.

Levenson, *The Secret Epidemic*.

1. Why was it already too late to stop the AIDS epidemic when the first cases were recognized? What factors helped to prolong the delayed response?

2. Why are vaccines based on dead viruses so much more dangerous than a vaccine based on viral fragments?

Autoimmunity—Self versus Self
Lecture 18

The immune system can be a fair-weather friend. When things are going well, we aren't even aware of all the microbial bullets that we're dodging until we the system fumbles and we get hit. In autoimmune diseases, however, the immune system turns on us, attacking our own cells as if we were our own enemy.

The acceptance of self, the body's own tissues, is called immunological **self-tolerance**. Usually, our bodies do a pretty good job of learning friend and foe. But sometimes this self-learning mechanism breaks down; then our friendly guard dog changes into a rabid beast, causing diseases like rheumatoid arthritis, multiple sclerosis, lupus, myasthenia gravis, and type 1 diabetes.

The whole idea of **autoimmune disease** might seem a little strange. Why hasn't natural selection weeded out those individuals whose immune systems can't make that critical distinction? In fact, autoimmunity isn't entirely a bad thing. **Self-reactive** B cells can be found throughout the blood in small numbers. It's as if the immune system needs to constantly challenge itself in order to stay sharp. However, a little challenge can go a very long way. Self-reactive cells are like ticking time bombs in the immune system.

A critical period for learning self versus nonself occurs very early in embryonic development. Every fetus is the product of 2 parents, which means every fetus has both parents' antigens on every cell, so the fetus

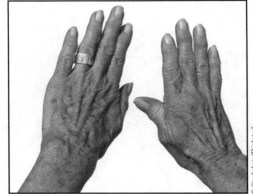

© iStockphoto/Thinkstock.

In rheumatoid arthritis, the body fails to recognize its own cells and attacks itself.

must tolerate both sets. Mothers have to acquire maternal-fetal tolerance so the fetus isn't attacked in the womb as an invader, possibly causing a miscarriage.

It's not enough to nip those self-reactive cells in the bud while we're still babies; adaptive immunity is a lifelong learning process. The immune system has to police every new generation of T cells as we grow. The bone marrow and thymus winnow out self-reactive and nonreactive B and T cells, respectively, before they are released into the body.

There are genetic predispositions and environmental triggers to certain autoimmune diseases, but the details are very poorly understood.

When self-tolerance fails and the immune system reacts to its own antigens, we may be witnessing the strategy of an agent provocateur—a microbe provoking the immune system into triggering an autoimmune response. Common microbes that can cause an autoimmune response include those of the genera *Syphilis*, *Chlamydia*, *Salmonella*, *Shigella*, *Staphylococcus*, and *Borrelia*.

Molecular mimicry may be the missing link between microbial infection and autoimmune diseases. A bacterial antigen could be similar enough to one of our own that the immune system attacks both microbe and body cells. Even after the microbe is gone, the self-reactive cells may continue to attack us. Molecular mimicry is the main, although not the only, suspect in multiple sclerosis and rheumatoid arthritis.

Is molecular mimicry the result of a shared cellular heritage, or is it a clever strategy evolved by microbes? We just don't know. There are so many different kinds of autoimmune diseases that it's hard to find any patterns. We know, for example, that there are genetic predispositions and environmental triggers to certain autoimmune diseases, but the details are very poorly understood. We also know that 75 percent of people with autoimmune diseases are female, so we assume there is a hormonal connection as well.

One recently discovered common thread is the superantigen (SAg). SAgs are antigens that activate many different kinds of T cells. A normal antigen will activate 1 in 10,000 to 1 in 1,000,000 T cells; a SAg will activate 1 in 50. Unfortunately, they also seem to reactivate the silenced clones of self-reactive cells, flooding the body with cells that are self-reactive to many different tissues. This would explain why some autoimmune diseases can affect so many different parts of the body at the same time.

The damage done in lupus, rheumatoid arthritis, and some other autoimmune diseases is done by the accumulation of the immune complex—a cluster of interlocked antibodies and antigens. Macrophages usually eat these byproducts, but in autoimmune disease, the macrophages can't keep up because the supply is essentially unlimited, so they remain in the body, causing tissue damage. The causes of other autoimmune diseases are even more mysterious; many genetic and environmental factors may be involved.

There are no treatments for most autoimmune diseases, though a wide variety of immunosuppressants and anti-inflammatory drugs are commonly prescribed. For most autoimmune diseases, all we can do is try to treat the symptoms. ■

Important Terms

autoimmune disease: The failure of the immune system to properly distinguish self from nonself, causing the immune system to attack the body's own cells and tissues.

molecular mimicry: The similarity between epitopes in our cells and those in various microbes, probably resulting from a shared genetic heritage; these similarities may be exploited as a microbial strategy.

self-tolerance: The immune system's tolerance for the body's own cells.

self-reactive cell: An immune system cell that reacts to the body's own cells as if they were foreign.

Lecture 18: Autoimmunity—Self versus Self

74

Suggested Reading

Albert and Inman, "Molecular Mimicry and Autoimmunity."

Fehervari and Sakaguchi, "Peacekeepers of the Immune System."

Lagerkvist, *Pioneers of Microbiology and the Nobel Prize.*

Questions to Consider

1. Why do we keep the same relative risk of getting multiple sclerosis that we had when we were a child if we move to a region where the risk is different?

2. What could explain molecular mimicry—an unfortunate resemblance between body cell epitopes and viral or bacterial epitopes—other than sheer (and improbable) coincidence?

Allergies and Asthma
Lecture 19

Allergies and asthma are immune system overreactions to harmless foreign substances. For some, they are a seasonal nuisance; for others, they can be life threatening. The culprit is immunoglobulin E—an antibody that lives in mucus membranes and can cause local or body-wide inflammation.

The word "**allergy**" comes from the Greek *allos* ("other") and *ergon* ("work" or "action"). In medical terms, refers to hypersensitivity to any foreign substance to which most people don't react, called an **allergen**. When the term was coined in 1906 by Dr. Clemens von Pirquet, allergies were rare, almost fashionable—a rich person's disorder.

Immunology was a brand-new field in Pirquet's day. His contemporaries Paul Ehrlich and Emil von Behring won the first Nobel Prize in Medicine in 1901 for curing diphtheria with blood serum—antibody-carrying blood from which the blood cells and clotting factors have been removed. Some of their patients developed serum sickness; their immune systems became hypersensitive to the serum—that is, they developed an allergy to it.

People who suffer from allergies are called atopic. **Atopy** is hereditary. If either parent is atopic, you have a 25 percent greater risk of being atopic yourself. If both parents are atopic, your risk goes up to 50 percent. Some 50–60 million Americans suffer from allergies; about 1 in 5 in the developed world have allergies.

For many people, allergies are a serious medical problem, requiring regular injections and avoidance of certain foods, objects, or environments. An allergen with a mild effect on one person could be fatal to another. **Anaphylaxis**, a whole-body inflammatory reaction, is the most severe form of allergic reaction. Symptoms can include respiratory problems, vomiting, diarrhea, hives, and loss of bladder control. Blood pressure drops so quickly that victims sometimes slip into shock and die.

In anaphylaxis, the first contact with the allergen causes a reaction. This so-called sensitizing dose causes the immune system to overreact if it encounters that same allergen later on—the shocking dose. Researchers are experimenting with exposing bee venom–sensitive to increasingly large amounts of bee venom and reduced the chance of shock to 2 percent after 3 to 5 years of regular treatment. This type of therapy is called desensitization.

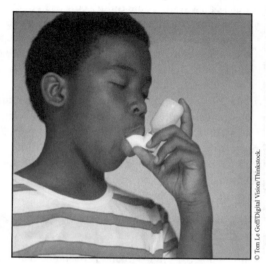

Desensitization depends on 2 antibodies: immunoglobulin G (**IgG**) and immunoglobulin E (**IgE**). IgG makes up roughly 75–80 percent of all antibodies in circulation at any one time; they fight viruses and bacteria. IgE antibodies are found in the skin, mucous membranes, and lungs; they're best at handling allergens like pollen, fungal spores, or parasitic worms. Small doses of IgG provoke a

Asthma may be a disease of civilization. The immune system overreacts to minor threats because it has too few major ones to combat.

low-level immune response, and continued doses can gradually override the more hypersensitive IgE response.

There is relatively little IgE in the body compared to the IgG—roughly a ratio of 1 to 100,000—but this tiny amount of IgE can do an incredible amount of damage. IgE stimulates mast cells to release **histamine**, triggering an inflammatory response, leading to itching, a runny nose, and so forth.

Allergies are on the increase worldwide; one theory behind this is our lifestyle in the developed world, living in airtight homes filled with objects that retain allergens, like upholstered furniture, carpets, drapes, bedding, mattresses, and stuffed animals. Surrounded by allergens from an early age, we become sensitized. This so-called hygiene hypothesis is still a bit controversial, but there are interesting statistics behind it.

Asthmatics have unusually high levels of IgE in their blood and are hypersensitive to common allergens, stress, and exercise. During an asthma attack, airways become tightly constricted, causing wheezing. Severe attacks can require hospitalization and can even be fatal. Like allergies, asthma diagnoses have risen over the past several decades. The incidence of asthma and allergies may continue to increase in the near future due to rising levels of carbon dioxide in the atmosphere.

The current approach to treating allergies and asthma is almost entirely pharmaceutical; there's little emphasis on environmental intervention and control, although that approach might offer more hope. Asthma in particular may be a disease of civilization. Individuals with heavy loads of parasitic worms—which we think IgE evolved to combat—rarely get asthma. IgE may be overreacting to various allergens because it has no worms to combat. ∎

Important Terms

allergen: Any environmental substance that provokes an allergic reaction.

allergy: Hypersensitivity to a foreign substance to which most people do not react.

anaphylaxis: A severe type 1 hypersensitivity reaction; it can lead to anaphylactic shock, in which widespread "leakage" in fine blood vessels results in a rapid drop in blood pressure and a critical condition.

atopy: Susceptibility to allergies.

histamine: An inflammatory cytokine produced by mast cells and cells called basophils that causes capillaries (tiny blood vessels) to dilate, which in turn increases blood flow and lets lymphocytes and defensive proteins get to the site of the injury. As a result, the injured area becomes red and swollen and feels warm to the touch.

IgE and **IgG:** Two immunoglobulins (Ig) that lie at the heart of the allergic reaction. IgG antibodies, which make up about 75–80 percent of the antibodies in circulation, are good for fighting viruses and bacteria, and IgE antibodies, found in skin, mucous membranes, and the lungs, are best at handling allergens like pollen, fungal spores, and parasitic worms.

Suggested Reading

Adams, *The Asthma Sourcebook.*

Jackson, *Allergy.*

Questions to Consider

1. Is raising children in clean and airtight houses in artificial urban environments a good idea from the standpoint of the immune system?

2. Why does our immune system overreact to such an extreme when we experience a bad attack of asthma?

Microbes as Weapons
Lecture 20

Biological and biochemical warfare are as old as human conflict. What humans lack in natural weapons—no fangs, no claws, no venom—we've made up for by using our intellect to imitate the adaptations of all the other predators.

Animals fight with horns, hooves, tooth, and claw; Plants fight quieter battles, as do fungi and bacteria, using exotic chemical compounds to stop an enemy in its tracks. Humans don't have sharp fangs nor slashing claws, but we can forge knives and swords. We can't secrete venom but can borrow venom from other animals.

We know that the use of animal venom as a weapon goes back at least as far as classical Greece. Homer describes warriors using poisoned spears and arrows in his epic poems. In legend, Hercules used the Hydra's venom to poison arrows to slay the centaur Nessus; later, that same poison was used

Just as animals constantly struggle against each other for dominance, so humans have adopted the tools of animals to fight each other.

to kill Hercules. Hannibal, the Carthaginian general, bombarded his enemy with clay pots full of poisonous snakes; meanwhile, the Romans did the same to their enemies with beehives.

Centuries before we had any inkling of the existence of microscopic creatures, we were using them in combat. The first known use of germ warfare occurred during the Anatolian War, around 1320–1318 B.C., when the Hittites drove sheep and donkeys infected with tularemia into enemy territory. Some 3000 years later, the Black Death entered Europe in a similar way. Turkish mercenaries besieging the Genoese army in the Crimean city of Caffa (modern-day Feodosiya) used catapults to launch plague-infected corpses into the city until the defenders sickened and died. The surviving Genoese soldiers scattered to ports all across the Mediterranean, bringing the Black Death with them.

The very first act of native-versus-colonist biological warfare in the New World may have been committed by a group of Iroquois. In the early 1700s, an angry tribe threw animal pelts into a stream used for drinking water by English troops, killing over 1000 soldiers. We know the British deliberately distributed smallpox-infected blankets to Native American tribes during the colonial era; the British may also have used smallpox against colonial troops and civilians during the American Revolution.

Smallpox was widespread in urbanized Europe; virtually everybody was exposed at an early age and developed immunity. Colonial America was comparatively rural and its populations isolated; many people had never been exposed to the disease. As rumors of British germ warfare tactics arose, George Washington decided to **inoculate** incoming recruits to the Continental Army; despite his caution, at one point about a third of his army was down with smallpox or with the inoculation. This tiny little virus nearly cost us the Revolutionary War; an outbreak certainly cost us the Battle of Quebec in December 1775 when the British commander, Sir Guy Carleton, used the germ against the colonial troops.

These crude tactics of our ancestors pale before our modern-day ability to cultivate the deadliest microbes on the planet. In World War I, gas was the preferred biological weapon: Gas attacks by the Germans caused

91,000 Allied casualties and an unknown number of German casualties from Allied counterattacks. The Germans also employed a limited form of biological warfare in World War I, cultivating anthrax and a cattle disease called glanders, which a German spy named Dr. Anton Casimir Dilger brought to Washington DC in 1915 in an unsuccessful attempt to destroy America's horse population. The Nazis ran a secret germ warfare program in World War II, experimenting with malaria, hepatitis A, and *Rickettsia* bacteria.

These crude tactics of our ancestors pale before our modern-day ability to cultivate the deadliest microbes on the planet.

The use of chemical and biological weapons was outlawed by the Geneva Protocol of 1925, but possession and research remained legal, so this provision was essentially toothless. What's more, the Geneva Protocol arguably started our modern biological arms race. It gave a Japanese microbiologist named Shiro Ishii the idea that biological weapons might actually be both feasible and very powerful. Ishii became the mastermind behind the Japanese biological weapons program. His tool kit included cholera, typhus, dysentery, salmonella, typhoid fever, botulin toxin, gangrene, smallpox, tuberculosis, and anthrax. The death toll from Ishii's experiments and attacks is estimated at over 400,000 people.

For many reasons, anthrax has been a perennial favorite in every nation's biological arsenal and has been recently adopted as a tool of bioterrorism. Caused by the bacterium *Bacillus anthracis*, its symptoms begin with a cough and progress to shortness of breath, high fever, convulsions, bleeding from bodily orifices, and a rapid and painful death within 12–24 hours of exposure. What is more, anthrax spores can remain viable for up to 40–80 years in soil, allowing anthrax to be highly virulent.

The U.S. chemical and germ program officially began in 1942 under the auspices of the Chemical Warfare Service (CWS), later called the Army Chemical Corps, but several sources allege that clandestine biowarfare research was already well underway in 1941. The program was centered at Fort Detrick, the Army Medical Research Institute of Infectious Diseases, where it is still located today. Britain and Canada later joined the program. In 1942, the British military used Gruinard Island, off the coast of Scotland, to test anthrax; it devastated the tiny island and even crossed to the mainland. It took 47 years to clean up the mess. ■

Important Term

inoculation: Introduction of a serum or vaccine into the body of an animal.

Suggested Reading

Harris, *Factories of Death.*

Koenig, *The Fourth Horseman.*

Mayor, *Greek Fire, Poison Arrows, and Scorpion Bombs.*

Questions to Consider

1. Does Lord Amherst really deserve the blame for the incident in which native Americans were given blankets infected with smallpox?

2. Are we ever justified in developing biological weapons, even as a deterrent?

Pandora's Box
Lecture 21

Following World War II, the United States and the Soviet Union launched massive germ warfare research programs; today, both nations and non-state militants have access to deadly microbial weapons. This threat raises many questions, from the practical (What can we do to prepare for biological attacks?) to the ethical (Is it right to arm ourselves with bioweapons?).

As we've seen, biowarfare is probably as ancient as warfare itself. There's no better example of this than the 2002 decision of India's defense ministry to perform modern research on the substances described in the ancient Indian text *Arthashastra*. Some of these formulas are said to help night vision and fight hunger and fatigue, but it also contains lists of snake, insect, and plant poisons, including detailed instructions for their preparation and use.

The American and Soviet germ warfare research programs were among the worst-kept secrets of the Cold War. Both the Americans and the Russians developed an anthrax bomb during the war; after, emphasis shifted from weapons production to research—especially field testing. In September 1950, the U. S. Navy bombarded San Francisco with a supposedly harmless bacteria and measured the bacteria's progress through the city's population.

We now know that bacterium, *Serratia marcescens*, which causes that pink slime found on bathroom tiles, is harmful, causing low-level infections like conjunctivitis and urinary tract infections, as well as more serious ones like meningitis and pneumonia. Nobody knows how many similar attacks were made on the U.S. population by its own government.

By the late 1960s, both the United States and Soviet Union had stockpiled several tons of biological weapons. In 1972, a new international treaty was written to replace the 1925 Geneva Protocol: the **Biological Weapons Convention (BWC)**. To date, 163 countries have ratified it, although Israel still refuses to sign. The BWC declared that "bacteriological methods of warfare" must be stopped, because using such weapons "would be repugnant to the conscience of mankind." However, it makes no provision for inspections; it prefers to rely on the honor system.

It didn't take long for the Soviets to violate the treaty; the head of their biowarfare program, Dr. Kanatjan Alibekov, defected to the United States in 1992 and revealed, among other frightening statistics, that the Soviet program employed 30,000 scientists and had engineered a strain of plague that was totally resistant to every known antibiotic.

For better or worse, microbes don't make particularly good weapons. They're too unpredictable, too hard to control.

The U.S. military concluded that if the Russians were violating the treaty, it was all right to do the same. Under President Ronald Reagan, the federal government officially spent $100 million a year under on developing biological weapons—and that's just what was on the books. American stockpiles included tularemia, brucellosis, Q fever, and Venezuelan equine encephalomyelitis. America also stockpiled plant pathogens to use against crops and weaponized several toxins, including staphylococcal enterotoxin B, saxitoxin, ricin, and botulinum.

The U.S. Office of Technology Assessment reported in 1995 that 17 other nations were actively engaged in bioweapons research, including Iraq, Iran, Libya, Syria, North Korea, Taiwan, Israel, Egypt, Vietnam, Laos, Cuba, Bulgaria, India, South Korea, South Africa, China, and Russia. Among modern nations, the United States, Russia, and Iraq have had the most ambitious and well-developed programs.

For better or worse, microbes don't make particularly good weapons. They're too unpredictable, too hard to control. Neither side wants to be the first to use them for fear of reprisal; they're only effective in the hands of someone who has nothing to lose. In that sense, biological weapons are custom made for terrorists. They spread chaos, fear, and death, and they provide the most bang for the buck; microbes are cheap compared to nuclear and chemical weapons and don't require elaborate missile systems to disperse, just access to your enemy's air and water.

There are many ways to tamper **weaponize** microbes, even with common, normally harmless bacteria like *Escherichia coli*. You could try to create an MDR strain, to alter its surface structure, to increase its growth rate, reproductive rate, or virulence, or the amount or the potency of the toxin that it can produce. But your weapon's effectiveness will still depend on many random factors: weather, wind speed, humidity, dispersal location, and so on.

Bioweapons are the last resort of the desperate and the foolish. The bad news is there are a lot of desperate and foolish people out there. **Bioterrorism** has become a constant threat. During the past century, there have been at least 52 cases where biological weapons were sought, obtained, or used by bioterrorists, with almost 1000 victims and 9 deaths.

What can we do to prepare for bioweapon attacks? Surveillance and arrests are not enough. Mandatory vaccinations may be required, which, in the United States at least, may not go over well with the populace. Bioweapons also pose a moral dilemma: Whether we continue to develop these weapons or not, other nations and groups will. Does this make it right to arm ourselves with these same horrible weapons? ■

Important Terms

Biological Weapons Convention (BWC): A 1975 agreement extending from the 1925 Geneva Protocol that bans the production and stockpiling of biological agents for use as weapons.

bioterrorism: The use of biological weapons in terrorist activities.

weaponize: To convert or prepare a biological agent for use in warfare.

Suggested Reading

Cole, *Clouds of Secrecy*.

Mangold and Goldberg, *Plague Wars*.

Questions to Consider

1. If all organisms have a right to life, should we prevent the extinction of species like the polio virus or the smallpox virus?

2. What aspects of microorganisms makes them less than ideal as weapons?

Old World to New
Lecture 22

Columbus, de Soto, and Cortés carried deadly Old World microbes to the New World, bringing about the destruction of some of the greatest civilizations this world has ever known. It wasn't just the guns, armor, and horses that defeated the Native Americans; Europeans were able to conquer the Americas because of the microbes they brought with them.

While the **Columbian Exchange** brought many American crops to the Old World, such as tomatoes and chocolate, as far as diseases go it was a very one-sided affair. Why didn't European explorers bring devastating virgin soil epidemics back from the New World? Part of the answer may lie in the domestication of animals.

Many of our worst Old World epidemic diseases came from domestic animals, but the New World had relatively few species that could be domesticated. Most of the large animals in North and South America were wiped out by the end of the Pleistocene, some 12,000 years ago. Paul Martin, a prominent geoscientist, claimed that this extinction event was due to the first organized human hunting.

The most abundant large New World mammal was the buffalo—the American bison. Buffalo were so abundant, you didn't need to domesticate them. If you wanted one, you just went out back and got one. The only New World animals available for domestication were llamas, alpacas, guinea pigs, turkeys, Muscovy ducks, and dogs. None of these animals were kept in large numbers and none were used for milk.

The Old World had much greater diversity of animals for domestication, as well as a much larger land area, than the New World. Our large herds of cattle and flocks of poultry became giant incubators for new strains. Century after century of constant and intimate contact with animals gave these microbes ample opportunity to jump from cattle or poultry to humans. Among the diseases that made the leap are measles, tuberculosis, influenza, whooping cough, and malaria.

Agriculture turned out to be a microbial bonanza in the Old World, too. It provided microbes with new habitats, new dispersal routes, and new hosts. Meanwhile, it allowed us to build up dense urban populations, which made us sitting ducks for **crowd diseases** like flu and smallpox.

None of these Old World diseases existed in the New World. Native Americans were a naïve population, and many virgin soil epidemics swept through the population: smallpox, measles, tuberculosis, flu, typhus, malaria, diphtheria, mumps, yellow fever, and plague. The New World population, estimated at roughly 20 million at the time of European contact, declined by more than 90 percent during the century following Columbus's voyage.

The first waves of colonists brought with them at least partial immunity to smallpox from centuries of exposure in Europe. But as time went on, more naïve populations emerged, especially in isolated rural areas, where crowd diseases quickly reach a dead end. Then, as American settlements grew larger, they reached a critical mass where smallpox and similar diseases could return in waves.

Buffalo were so abundant in pre-Columbian America that they were easy to hunt; thus the natives had no need to domesticate them.

One of the unsung heroes of the colonial smallpox epidemics was Cotton Mather. Most people know him as the stern and implacable inquisitor of the colonial witch trials; however, he was also a well-respected scholar and a member of the Royal Society of London. Mather had heard about inoculation in 1706 from a slave who had received it as a child in Africa. Mather became a champion of inoculation in the colonies and experimented successfully with **variation**, which uses live smallpox virus, in several patients.

Smallpox is caused by the *Variola* virus, a DNA virus and one of the largest viruses known. It's a member of the Orthopox family, which includes smallpox, cowpox, camelpox, gerbilpox, and monkeypox. It spreads via aerosol dispersal, entering a new host through the nose or mouth. The first symptoms appear in about 10–12 days—high fever, intense headaches, and backaches, followed by a characteristic rash. The fatality rate ranges between 1 and 30 percent; there is no effective treatment once the first full-blown symptoms appear. You either survive or you die.

As American settlements grew larger, they reached a critical mass where smallpox and similar diseases could return in waves.

Despite its historic ravages, smallpox turned out to be relatively easy to control. Victims are highly infective, but for only about a week after the onset of the rash. Smallpox requires close exposure to spread, so quarantine in the early stages is very highly effective. It's a very stable virus, unlike the flu virus, which makes it much easier to eliminate by a simple vaccination. This stability might also explain why it never has coevolved into a more benign strain.

Mather's variolation could prevent smallpox, but it was dangerous. It fell to a British country doctor named Edward Jenner to develop the first safe vaccine in 1796. His inoculation was made from **pus** from a milkmaid's cowpox sores—cowpox being a nondeadly infection in humans that conferred immunity to its cousin smallpox. The word "vaccination," in fact, comes from the Latin *vacca*, meaning "cow," for this reason.

Thanks to Jenner, smallpox is no longer the scourge of civilization. A series of global initiatives begun in the 1950s by the United Nations World Health Organization officially eradicated smallpox in December 1979. This was the first time in history that the human race took aim at a single microorganism, with the sole intent of wiping it out of existence, and won. ∎

Important Terms

Columbian Exchange: The exchange of trade goods, cultures, ideas, crops, livestock, and diseases between the Old World and the New World following the voyage of Columbus.

crowd disease: A disease that requires a dense population to sustain itself.

pus: A mixture of dead and dying neutrophils, microbes, and body cells that forms at the site of an infection.

variolation: Intentionally introducing smallpox into a human body to provide immunity.

Suggested Reading

Crosby, *The Columbian Exchange*.

Diamond, *Guns, Germs, and Steel*.

Martin, *Twilight of the Mammoths*.

Questions to Consider

1. Why do we rarely catch diseases directly from other animals, yet many of our worst human diseases came from animals?

2. Why was smallpox such a big problem for the American colonists when so many of their parents and grandparents were born in Europe, where immunity to smallpox was relatively common?

Close Encounters of the Microbial Kind
Lecture 23

When we voyage into the final frontier of outer space, will our bacterial hitchhikers find alien races waiting for their deadly microbial sting? Or will we bring back an alien microbe that will spell doom for the human race? In fact, microscopic creatures could make our long journey to the stars possible and help turn our destination into a new Eden.

We live our lives surrounded by millions of creatures as alien to us as we are to an ant. Take the curious case of the bacterium that wasn't. Bacteria are primitive cells called **prokaryotes** with rigid cell walls, no nuclei, and a single loop of DNA, with many of their important genes carried on plasmids. For many years we thought all prokaryotes were alike.

Using the new tools of DNA analysis, microbiologist Carl Woese discovered in the late 1970s that some bacteria weren't bacteria at all. He named them archaebacteria, later shortened to **archaea**, Greek for "ancient things." They were a totally different kind of microscopic life, as distantly related to bacteria as bacteria are to man.

Archaeans form 1 of the 3 domains of living things: Bacteria, Archaea, and **Eukarya**—which include the plants, animals, fungi, algae, and protozoa. We're actually more closely related to the archaeans than we are to bacteria. They're like prokaryotic bacteria in their basic morphology and metabolism, but their genetic control system and protein synthesis mechanism are more like a eukaryotic cell—our cells. They were first called **extremophiles** because they often live in unusual and extreme environments. Now we know that they're common and abundant in a wide variety of habitats.

Archaeans' ability to cope with the most extreme environments makes them a model organism for microbial life on an alien planet. But what are the odds of encountering alien life? If we're talking about intelligent life, the odds may be very small. But if we're talking about microbes, the odds are much, much higher.

In 1953, a graduate student named Stanley Miller demonstrated how easily a random combination of chemicals can almost accidentally form complex organic molecules. Miller mixed water with methane, ammonia, and hydrogen, and he passed electric sparks through the mixture to imitate lightning strikes. Within 2 days, amino acids were forming in the mixture. The Miller-Urey experiments, as they came to be called, have since created all 20 amino acids found in living cells, all 5 nucleotide bases in DNA and RNA, and fatty acids—the precursors of cell membranes. Given that the same raw ingredients of Earth's microbes are common throughout the universe, the Miller-Urey experiments greatly increase the chances of microbial aliens.

© Digital Vision/Thinkstock.

Some scientists argue that life on Earth may have been seeded by bacteria carried on an asteroid from Mars.

Many people have since abandoned Miller's model in favor of a CO_2/ neutral model. Neutral models base their chemistry on a carbon dioxide, nitrogen, and water atmosphere, which is actually a much more probable starting point for Earth's atmosphere, and one that relies on very heavy volcanic activity. Another alternative hypothesis for the origins of life on earth points out that cosmic dust clouds are vast synthetic factories for an astonishing array of organic compounds. The early bombardment of Earth by comets, which may have been the source of most of our planet's water, would also have added large amounts of organic material to the primordial soup.

Panspermia is the theory that life was seeded on Earth and other planets from outer space. We think the idea originated with the Greek philosopher Anaxagoras, although similar ideas are found all the way back in the ancient Hindu Vedas. Francis Crick, the co-discoverer of DNA, and Leslie Orgel proposed what they called **directed panspermia**, the theory that life was intentionally seeded on Earth and other planets by an intelligent race of aliens or their robotic probes.

We already know that Earth's microbes are hardy enough to survive for long periods of time in outer space, especially if they're embedded in a solid object, like a rock or a piece of space equipment. If we are truly the descendants of alien microbes, then an alien virus or bacterium might be able to start the ultimate virgin soil pandemic, possibly bringing about the end of humanity.

Life on Earth could actually have begun with the arrival of microbes from Mars.

A Martian meteorite called ALH84001, found in Antarctica's Allan Hills, might contain tiny microbial fossils, or nanofossils. Most scientists have dismissed the nanofossils as human contamination, but NASA's closer examination of the rock in 2009 has reopened the issue. This new study found evidence that the rock had been exposed to liquid water on Mars. We may, in fact, be looking at fossils of a microbial life form from another planet. The rock itself is over 4 billion years old, which raises an interesting possibility: We might be Martians. Life on Earth could actually have begun with the arrival of microbes from Mars.

Mars seems a dead planet today, but can we bring it back to life? The logical way to try would be with **cyanobacteria**, or blue-green algae, the microbe that invented **photosynthesis** some 4 billion years ago. Cyanobacteria created Earth's oxygen atmosphere as a waste product, changing the basic chemistry of the planet to an oxidizing environment. This so-called **oxygen revolution** allowed eukaryotic cells, the oxygen-using cells that we are made from, to replace prokaryotic cells, the cells bacteria and archaeans are made from, as the dominant organisms on Earth in terms of size and complexity. ∎

Important Terms

archaea (sing. **archaean**): Primitive prokaryotic cells that share a common ancestor with members of the domain Eukarya; when capitalized, refers to one of the 3 taxonomic domains of living things.

cyanobacteria: Formerly called blue-green algae, a diverse group of bacteria that evolved photosynthesis nearly 3 billion years ago.

directed panspermia: The theory that life was intentionally seeded on Earth by an alien race, either directly or through robotic probes.

Eukarya: One of the 3 domains of living things; Eukarya include plants, animals, fungi, and protists (algae and protozoa).

extremophile: A microorganism (bacterium or archaean) that is adapted to live in extreme environmental conditions.

oxygen revolution: The creation of the oxygen atmosphere by ancient cyanobacteria and the many chemical and biological changes that resulted from this fundamental alteration of planetary chemistry.

panspermia: The theory that life was seeded on Earth from outer space.

photosynthesis: The synthesis of glucose from water and carbon dioxide through the use of light energy, producing atmospheric oxygen as a byproduct.

Suggested Reading

Boss, *The Crowded Universe*.

Cooper, *The Search for Life on Mars*.

Davies, *The Fifth Miracle*.

Ward and Brownlee, *Rare Earth*.

Questions to Consider

1. What do you think of the theory of panspermia? If you think such a thing is possible, do think accidental or directed panspermia is more likely?

2. In what ways do extremophiles serve as valuable models for life in outer space?

Microbes as Friends
Lecture 24

By now, you may be thinking microbes are all bad guys. Nothing could be further from the truth. Bacteria literally created the world we know today; they continue to make life as we know it both possible and pleasurable.

Only about 1400 species of the million or so microbes that we know about are harmful. Imagine a world without good wine or beer, a world without chocolate, a world without oxygen. We wouldn't even exist were it not for the microscopic life that preceded us.

We carry the ghosts of distant bacterial ancestors in our genes, ancestors who harnessed the power of the Sun, created the world's first ecosystem, and even changed the chemistry of the planet. We might even use them to make a better tomorrow.

The first reports from 2010's *Deepwater Horizon* oil spill horrified the world—the beautiful Gulf of Mexico, its coastline and islands, all soaked in oil. Yet by the summer of 2010, much of the damage, at least to the naked eye, had disappeared. This isn't to the credit of BP and their repeated failures to cap the well but to hungry bacteria. Dr. Terry Hazen, a microbial ecologist at the Lawrence Berkeley National Laboratory, found that underwater microbes were not only gobbling up the oil but doing it much, much faster than anybody had anticipated.

Cleaning up oil spills is just one of the many ways that bacteria can be used in **bioremediation**—that is, using natural organisms to decontaminate polluted environments. Bacteria are especially good at breaking down human sewage, industrial toxic waste, and the chlorinated hydrocarbons from which pesticides are made.

Bacteria can also be used in engineering and industry. For example, many bacteria and archaeans live in and naturally extract minerals from ores, including copper, uranium, and gold. Using microorganisms to process ore is not only cheaper than traditional methods; it also does much less environmental damage. About 25 percent of the world's copper is currently obtained through **biomining**.

When we study bacteria in the lab, we usually study them in a liquid suspension. But in nature, bacteria more often occur in thin sheets called **biofilms**. Bacteria in biofilms can behave very differently than bacteria in liquid suspension. For instance, bacteria in biofilms may be more resistant to antibiotics. The study of biofilms is at the cutting edge of modern microbiology.

Microbes also make the world a tastier place to live in.

Biofilms of cyanobacteria formed column-like groupings called **stromatolites**, which led to the oxygen revolution. The oxygen revolution in turn led to a biological revolution, because a more efficient type of cell soon evolved to take advantage of those higher levels of oxygen in the air—**Eukarya**. All higher organisms, including microscopic algae and protozoa, are made of eukaryotic cells.

Bacteria can be used as targeted and environmentally friendly **biological controls** in place of broad spectrum pesticides. *Bacillus thuringiensis* is used against caterpillars, and the subspecies *B. thuringiensis israelensis* is used to kill black flies, which carry the nematodes whose gut bacteria cause river blindness (onchocerciasis), which currently affects 37 million people worldwide. *Bacillus popilliae* and *Bacillus lentimorbus* have been used since the 1940s to control Japanese beetle infestations. A virus is used to kill the rhinoceros beetles that attack coconut palms throughout the South Pacific.

Microbes also make the world a tastier place to live in. Part of the complex taste of chocolate is due to the bacterial fermentation of the seeds from which chocolate is made. Bacterial fermentation also causes the stink in Limburger cheese, courtesy of *Brevibacterium linens*, and *Propionibacterium freudenreichii* puts the holes in Swiss cheese. Yeast, a microscopic fungus, is responsible for the primary fermentation of wine and bacteria for malolactic fermentation, which mellows too-acidic wines.

Yeast is also used in beer making, and a scientist named Vladimir Baibakov has discovered that adding *Bifidobacteria* to beer slows down oxidation. The bacteria absorb traces of detergents and heavy metal from the brewing process and allow the beer to function as a **probiotic**. This makes **bifidobeer** a better-tasting and much healthier brew.

Bacteria could also be used to help protect babies from AIDS. A team at the University of Madrid recently isolated several species of bacteria in breast milk that can inhibit infections of HIV-1 up to 55 percent. That study explains the puzzling fact that breastfed babies do not tend to get AIDS from their HIV-positive mothers. It remains to be seen whether the bacteria are effective in isolation or only work as part of breast milk.

Dr. Dorothy Matthews found that mice fed a common soil bacterium, *Mycobacterium vaccae*, complete lab mazes at twice the speed of control mice and showed significantly less stress in the testing environment. As it turns out, these bacteria activate a group of neurons in the brain that secrete serotonin. Cancer patients treated with the bacteria show much lower depression scores than the average patient.

The long road of coevolution with our constant microscopic companions has changed our bodies, our history, and our world. Where the future of men and microbes is concerned, we're only limited by our imagination. I hope this series of lectures has given you a new perspective on the invisible world that surrounds us. Solving the mysteries of the microscopic world will not be easy, but learning more about our microbial partners will make the world our children inherit a better place to live. ■

Important Terms

bioremediation: The use of natural organisms to decontaminate polluted environments.

bifidobeer: Beer prepared with bifidobacteria, which are a common gut bacteria that aid in digestion.

biofilm: A thin sheet or mat of bacteria held together by a sticky substance on their cell walls. Bacteria growing in biofilms can behave differently from those grown in suspension.

biological control: The use of natural organisms and processes instead of chemical pesticides to control common pest species (for example, using *Thuringen* bacteria against caterpillars).

biomining: Exploiting the natural reactions of microorganisms, many of which leach metals from ores, as a tool for mineral extraction.

bioremediation: The use of natural organisms to decontaminate polluted environments.

probiotic: A commercial preparation containing beneficial bacteria as a dietary supplement.

stromatolite: A thick, column-shaped mound formed by many layers of cyanobacteria biofilms; a dominant feature of Earth for 100 million years and its first true ecosystem.

Suggested Reading

Davidson, *Big Fleas Have Little Fleas*.

Margulis and Sagan, *Microcosmos*.

Sachs, *Good Germs, Bad Germs*.

Questions to Consider

1. Can you think of some of the ways we teach our children, by word or action, about the microbial world that might predispose them to consider all microbes as bad or dangerous?

2. In what 2 fundamental ways do we carry the ghosts of our bacterial ancestors in our cells?

Glossary

acidophile: An acid-loving extremophile; specifically, bacteria and archaeans that thrive in extremely acid environments like sulfuric pools and geysers or acid mine drainage.

activation: The process by which helper T cells can trigger B cells to start producing antibodies and memory cells. *See also* **cellular immune response** and **presentation**.

adaptive immunity: A type of immunity evolved by higher animals that doesn't look for general patterns of shared structure but rather for minute differences in molecules shared by hosts and microbes. *See also* **innate immunity**.

allele: A variant form of a gene.

allergen: Any environmental substance that provokes an allergic reaction.

allergic reaction: An inflammatory response to an allergen, usually involving itchiness, redness, swelling, hives, or runny nose—symptoms collectively called type 1 hypersensitivity. *See* **IgE and IgG antibodies**.

allergy: Hypersensitivity to a foreign substance to which most people do not react.

anaphylaxis: A severe type 1 hypersensitivity reaction; it can lead to anaphylactic shock, in which widespread "leakage" in fine blood vessels results in a rapid drop in blood pressure and a critical condition.

antibiotic: Any substance that either kills microbes outright or slows down their population growth.

antibiotic resistance: The evolutionarily acquired ability of microbes to either neutralize or withstand an antibiotic.

antibody: A protein that can attach to a corresponding epitope and flag a cell or molecule for destruction by the immune system. *See* **B cell** and **plasma cell**.

antigen: A fragment of a cell or protein that can be detected by the immune system; also, a molecule or cell with an epitope in its structure.

antigen receptors: Molecular binding sites on immune system cells that correspond to a particular antigen.

antigenic drift: A significant alteration in the structure of the surface proteins of a virus, effectively disguising it from the immune system. Usually refers to influenza, especially the structure of H spikes and N spikes.

antigenic shift: A dramatic alteration in the structure of the surface proteins of a virus sufficient to trigger an epidemic.

antigen-presenting cell (APC): Immune system cells that act as messengers by carrying antigens on their major histocompatability complex to the corresponding T cells for activation. APCs include macrophages, B cells, and dendritic cells.

arboreal: Adapted for living in and moving through trees. *See also* **cursorial**.

archaea (sing. **archaean**): Primitive prokaryotic cells that share a common ancestor with members of the domain Eukarya; when capitalized, refers to one of the 3 taxonomic domains of living things. *See* **bacteria, domain, Eukarya**.

argument from design: The claim that the order of the natural world could only have come into existence as a product of divine will and intelligent design. A central tenet of the modern-day intelligent design and creation science movements, but actually a very ancient argument.

astrobiology: The study of life beyond the Earth, also known as xenobiology or exobiology.

atopy: Susceptibility to allergies.

autoimmune disease: The failure of the immune system to properly distinguish self from nonself, causing the immune system to attack the body's own cells and tissues. *See* **self-tolerance**.

B cell: A type of lymphocyte whose function is to produce antibodies for specific antigens and to form memory cells to guard against any future encounters with that same antigen. *See also* **plasma cell** and **T cell**.

bacteria (sing. **bacterium**): Primitive unicellular organisms; when capitalized, refers to one of the 3 taxonomic domains of living things. *See* **archaea**, **domain**, **Eukarya**.

banded iron deposits: Dark layers or stripes in ancient rocks that were formed by oxygen from early cyanobacteria reacting with iron suspended in water, with the heavier iron oxides settling out of solution.

benign strain: A species or subspecies of microbe that is less harmful than competing strains of the same species.

bifidobeer: Beer prepared with bifidobacteria, which are a common gut bacteria that aid in digestion. *See* **probiotic**.

biofilm: A thin sheet or mat of bacteria held together by a sticky substance on their cell walls. Bacteria growing in biofilms can behave differently from those grown in suspension.

biological control: The use of natural organisms and processes instead of chemical pesticides to control common pest species (for example, using *Thuringen* bacteria against caterpillars).

Biological Weapons Convention (BWC): A 1975 agreement extending from the 1925 Geneva Protocol that bans the production and stockpiling of biological agents for use as weapons.

biomining: Exploiting the natural reactions of microorganisms, many of which leach metals from ores, as a tool for mineral extraction.

bioremediation: The use of natural organisms to decontaminate polluted environments.

bioterrorism: The use of biological weapons in terrorist activities.

blood type: The presence or absence of the A and B antigens on human blood cells.

catalyst: A chemical that takes part in or mediates a chemical reaction but is not altered by that reaction. A small amount of catalyst can catalyze many chemical reactions, making it invaluable in many industrial processes and in the control of complex processes like living systems. *See* **enzyme**.

cellular immune response: The presentation and activation of T cells in the immune system. *See also* **humoral immune response** and **primary immune response**.

cellular immunity: Actions of the immune system that involve macrophages, killer cells, and the release of cytokines but not antibodies or complement system proteins.

codon: A series of 3 genetic nucleotides that code for a particular amino acid. The sequence of codons determines the proper sequence of amino acids needed to assemble a particular protein.

coevolution: An evolutionary change in one organism that leads to an evolutionary change in another organism that interacts with it.

Columbian Exchange: The exchange of trade goods, cultures, ideas, crops, livestock, and diseases between the Old World and the New World following the voyage of Columbus.

commensalism: A form of symbiosis in which one partner is helped and the other is neither helped nor hindered, such as Spanish moss hanging on trees. *See also* **mutualism** and **parasitism**.

competition: A contest for resources that affects the birth rate or the death rate of 2 or more competing species. *See also* **interspecific competition**, **intraspecific competition**, **niche overlap**, and **realized niche**.

competitive exclusion: A situation in which one species or population outcompetes its rival to the point where the rival is locally eliminated.

complement system: A group of about 25 proteins found in blood or other bodily fluids that can build up on the surface of a microbe, starting a cascade reaction that punctures the microbe's cell wall. The complement system has a variety of other functions, including releasing chemicals to attract other immune cells and opsonization.

crowd disease: A disease that requires a dense population to sustain itself.

cryophile (a.k.a. **psychrophile**): A cold-loving extremophile; specifically, bacteria and archaeans that thrive in extremely cold environments like pack ice and the polar seas.

cursorial: Adapted for moving rapidly over the ground. *See also* **arboreal**.

cyanobacteria: Formerly called blue-green algae, a diverse group of bacteria that evolved photosynthesis nearly 3 billion years ago. *See also* **biofilm** and **stromatolite**.

cytokine: A molecule that mediates an interaction between cells. The immune response relies on many different types of cytokines. *See also* **histamine**, **inflammatory cell**, and **mast cell**.

cytokine storm: A cascade reaction of defensive proteins that can prove fatal—the immune system's equivalent of a thermonuclear attack.

cytotoxic cell: A type of defensive cell common to all animals that effectively stabs foreign cells to death by punching holes through their cell walls.

Darwinian medicine (a.k.a. **evolutionary medicine**): The consideration of traditional medical problems from an ecological and evolutionary perspective, focused on the coevolution of humans and pathogens.

dendritic cell: A type of lymphocyte in mammals that functions as an antigen-presenting cell, helping to bridge the gap between the innate and adaptive immune systems.

density-dependent limiting factor: A limiting factor whose effects are directly proportional to the density of a population, such as predation or disease.

density-independent limiting factor: A limiting factor whose effects are not proportional to population density, like bad weather or natural disasters.

diffusion: The movement of atoms and molecules from an area of higher concentration to an area of lower concentration.

directed panspermia: The theory that life was intentionally seeded on Earth by an alien race, either directly or through robotic probes. *See also* **panspermia**.

disturbance: Any force or factor that perturbs the normal functioning of an ecosystem.

DNA: Two strands of complementary nucleotides attached to a molecular backbone of sugar and phosphate molecules. The sequence of nucleotides codes for the synthesis of proteins. *See also* **RNA**.

DNA vaccine: Plasmids that code for a critical protein in the life cycle of a particular microbe.

domain: The highest level of biological classification. *See* **archaea**, **bacteria**, and **Eukarya**.

Drake equation: An equation proposed by astrophysicist Frank Drake that represents the number of alien civilizations in the galaxy that could communicate with us.

durability: The microbial strategy of persistence and dormancy for the long-term possibility of infection.

ecosystem: All of the biological communities in a given area, together with their physical habitat.

enzyme: A protein that can act as a chemical catalyst, mediating a reaction without being changed by it. Enzymes control the rate, direction, synthesis, and degradation of many biochemical reactions in the body. Most of what our genes actually code for are different kinds of enzymes.

epidemic: An outbreak of disease that exceeds the expected norm, usually applied to an infectious disease that appears suddenly and moves rapidly through a population. *See also* **pandemic**.

epidemiologic cycle: The demographic pattern of infection or mortality over time in a given population.

epitope: A fragment of protein from a cell or molecule that can be detected by the immune system. *See also* **antigen**.

Eukarya: One of the 3 domains of living things; Eukarya include plants, animals, fungi, and protists (algae and protozoa). *See also* **archaea** and **bacteria**.

eukaryote: A relatively advanced cell type characteristic of members of the domain Eukarya, with a cell nucleus and several cellular organelles constructed from membranes, such as mitochondria and chloroplasts. *See also* **prokaryote**.

evolution: A change in gene frequency over time; descent with modification from a common ancestor.

evolutionary arms race: The coevolution of 2 competing organisms, each of which must constantly adapt to changes in the strategies of the other; a kind of evolutionary one-upmanship.

extremophile: A microorganism (bacterium or archaean) that is adapted to live in extreme environmental conditions. *See also* **acidophile**, **cryophile**, **halophile**, and **thermophile**.

extrinsic limiting factor: A limiting factor that comes from outside the individual or population, such as sunlight, water, or nutrients. *See also* **intrinsic limiting factor**.

fermentation: An ancient metabolic pathway evolved by cells before the formation of an oxygen atmosphere. Fermentation produces alcohol as a byproduct. *See* **respiration**.

fundamental niche: The niche an organism occupies in the absence of competition; also called its theoretical niche. *See also* **realized niche**.

fusion inhibitor: A type of AIDS drug that prevents HIV from fusing with the surface of a cell to inject its contents.

germ theory: The theory that microorganisms were the cause of human diseases, finally established in the late 19th century. *See* **humors** and **miasma**.

Great Famine: A famine in Europe between 1315 and 1317 that claimed millions of lives.

halophile: A salt-loving extremophile; specifically, bacteria and archaeans that thrive in extremely saline environments like the Dead Sea.

helper T cell (a.k.a. T_H **or CD4+ cells**): A critical immune system T cell that, when activated, coordinates a wide range of immune processes through the secretion of messenger molecules called cytokines. *See also* **killer T cell**.

hemoglobin: The protein that binds oxygen to transport it throughout the circulatory system.

herd immunity: A complete or partial immunity in the surviving population (the remaining "herd") after an epidemic.

histamine: An inflammatory cytokine produced by mast cells and cells called basophils that causes capillaries (tiny blood vessels) to dilate, which in turn increases blood flow and lets lymphocytes and defensive proteins get to the site of the injury. As a result, the injured area becomes red and swollen and feels warm to the touch. *See also* **inflammatory cell**.

host manipulation: A microbial strategy in which the parasite alters host behavior in a way that significantly benefits the parasite.

host switching: The transfer of a parasite to a new primary host.

humoral response: Part of the primary immune response; the activation of B cells by helper T cells to make antibodies (plasma cells) and memory cells. *See also* **cellular immune response** and **plasma cell**.

humors: Bodily fluids whose imbalance was once thought to be the cause of human diseases. The 4 humors were black bile, yellow bile, phlegm, and blood. The theory of humors was inspired by the 4 elements of the ancient Greeks (earth, air, fire, and water). *See also* **germ theory** and **miasma**.

hunter-gatherer: A person who leads a nomadic lifestyle, living directly off the land, with no attempt to cultivate or domesticate food organisms.

hypermutability: The tendency of certain organisms, such as the influenza virus, to mutate at a relatively high rate. *See* **RNA virus**.

IgE and **IgG**: Two immunoglobulins (Ig) that lie at the heart of the allergic reaction. IgG antibodies, which make up about 75–80 percent of the antibodies in circulation, are good for fighting viruses and bacteria, and IgE antibodies, found in skin, mucous membranes, and the lungs, are best at handling allergens like pollen, fungal spores, and parasitic worms. *See also* **allergic reaction**.

immunity: Disease resistance acquired by exposure to a pathogen. The immune system "remembers" the encounter by keeping some antibodies around from each disease it defeats, in case the same pathogen returns. *See* **adaptive immunity** and **innate immunity**.

incubation period: Period of time between infection and the first symptoms of an infection. Sometimes called the latency period, although that term usually refers to the time between infection and becoming infectious to others.

inflammatory cell: A cell involved in the inflammatory response that is densely packed with granules loaded with potent chemical mediators like histamine. *See also* **cytokine** and **mast cell**.

innate immunity: A primitive type of immune system common to a wide variety of animals that gives certain cells the ability to identify foreign cells by recognizing patterns of sugar molecules in their cell walls. Phaogocytes, cytotoxic cells, and inflammatory cells are components of innate immunity. *See also* **adaptive immunity**.

inoculation: Introduction of a serum or vaccine into the body of an animal.

interstitial habitat: A habitat within and among the grains of soil in terrestrial or aquatic habitats.

intrinsic limiting factor: A limiting factor that operates from within the individuals of a population, affecting reproductive physiology or reproductive behavior. *See* **extrinsic limiting factor**.

iron withholding: Adaptive response in which the human body sequesters or binds iron so that it is not accessible to bacteria, for whom it is a limiting nutrient.

killer T cells (T_C or CD8+ cells): Cytotoxic T cells that are especially good at killing cells that are cancerous or have been infected with a virus. *See* **cytotoxic cell** and **helper T cell**.

Koch's postulates: A series of steps established by physician Robert Koch to prove that a particular microbe causes a particular disease.

leukocyte (a.k.a. **white blood cell**): An immune system cell that helps fight infectious diseases or foreign proteins. The presence and number of these cells is often used in the diagnosis of disease. White blood cell types include neutrophils, dendritic cells, lymphocytes, and macrophages.

limiting factor: Any force or factor that regulates the growth of a natural population. *See* **density-dependent limiting factor**, **density-independent limiting factor**, **extrinsic limiting factor**, and **intrinsic limiting factor**.

Little Ice Age: A 500-year climate aberration (A.D. 1350–1850) during which temperatures in Europe were significantly colder than normal; the period was characterized by extreme and intense weather, such as floods and droughts. *See also* **Medieval Warm Period**.

long-term nonprogressor: An HIV-positive individual who has avoided developing the symptoms of AIDS for 10 years or more.

lymph nodes: Small spherical organs of the immune system where B cells and T cells are concentrated in large numbers; the immune system equivalent of a garrison fort.

lymphatic system: A major part of the immune system consisting of a circulatory network containing a clear fluid called lymph, which carries a wide variety of cells involved in immunity, together with the structures associated with making and moving lymphocytes.

lymphocytes: Cells involved in adaptive immunity. *See* **B cell**, **natural killer cell**, and **T cell**.

macrophage: An immune cell common to most animals that "eats" pathogens. Macrophages can travel almost anywhere in the body, devour pathogens, and carry them to the lymph nodes to trigger an immune response.

magic bullet: Term coined by the physician Sir Alexander Fleming to refer to drugs that can target a particular type of bacteria.

mast cell: An inflammatory cell that releases the cytokine histamine.

Medieval Warm Period: A climate aberration preceding the Little Ice Age, during which average temperatures were significantly higher than normal. *See also* **Little Ice Age**.

memory cell: An activated B cell that is relatively long-lived and can be rapidly cloned if the same antigen or invader returns. *See also* **plasma cell**.

messenger RNA (mRNA): A form of RNA used in the synthesis of proteins that is assembled by matching complementary nucleotides (A/T, C/G) to replicate the sequence of nucleotides on a strand of DNA. *See also* **codon**, **ribosomal RNA (rRNA)**, and **transfer RNA (tRNA)**.

methanogens: A group of anaerobic archaeans that generate methane as a result of their metabolic processes. Found (among other places) as symbionts in the guts of cows and termites, where they help digest cellulose.

major histocompatability complex (MHC): A receptor site on the outside of every vertebrate cell that can hold onto an epitope or antigen so that immune system cells can recognize it. *See also* **antigen-presenting cell (APC)**.

miasma: A noxious vapor once believed to be the cause of human disease. *See* **germ theory** and **humors**.

microbe: Any organism small enough to require a microscope to clearly see it.

molecular mimicry: The similarity between epitopes in our cells and those in various microbes, probably resulting from a shared genetic heritage; these similarities may be exploited as a microbial strategy.

mutation: A random alteration of genetic information that can occur in RNA or DNA.

mutualism: A form of symbiosis in which both partners are helped by the relationship (the traditional meaning of symbiosis), such as a lichen, a fungus cooperating with a green algae or cyanobacteria. *See* **commensalism** and **parasitism**.

myelin sheath: A sheath insulating the nerves that is essential for the rapid conduction of nervous signals in vertebrates and is attacked in multiple sclerosis.

naïve population: An isolated population that has not been systematically exposed to an infectious disease. *See* **virgin soil epidemic**.

natural killer cell (NK cell): A cytotoxic cell that seeks out and destroys cells invaded by microbes; NK cells specialize in attacking cancerous cells or cells invaded by a virus.

natural killer T cell (NKT cell): A cell that acts like a regular natural killer cell but can also mediate adaptive immune responses by releasing messenger chemicals called cytokines.

natural theology: A school of philosophy that seeks to prove the existence of God through observing the natural world and through the use of human reason. Natural theologians maintained that the balance of nature and the exquisite fit between form and function were evidence of a divine plan behind nature.

neutrophil: A type of lymphocyte that specializes in attacking bacteria and fungi. They account for over half of the lymphocytes circulating in our bodies at any given time. *See also* **pus**.

niche: The functional role that an organism plays in an ecosystem; also, the sum total of a species's needs and the range of conditions within which it can survive.

niche overlap: The degree to which the needs of 2 competing species overlap one another, which determines the intensity of the competition between them.

nitrogen fixation: The enzymatic process by which bacteria fix atmospheric nitrogen into ammonium, a form that can be used by plants.

nonequilibrium theory: The idea that certain ecosystems are not harmed by disturbance but rather thrive on it.

nosocomial infection: A hospital-acquired infection.

nucleotide: A biomolecule whose many important functions include carrying the genetic code. The 4 nucleotides used in DNA are adenine, guanine, cytosine, and thymine (abbreviated A, G, C, and T). RNA substitutes uracil (U) for thymine (T). *See* **codon**.

oceanic conveyor belt: The pattern of global ocean currents that redistribute equatorial heat to the poles.

opsonization: Part of the complement system; a process through which an invading cell is coated with proteins that help phagocytes bind to them.

oxygen revolution: The creation of the oxygen atmosphere by ancient cyanobacteria and the many chemical and biological changes that resulted from this fundamental alteration of planetary chemistry. *See* **photosynthesis** and **stromatolite**.

pandemic: An epidemic that occurs over a wide geographic area.

panspermia: The theory that life was seeded on Earth from outer space. *See also* **directed panspermia**.

parasitism: A form of symbiosis in which one partner is helped and the other is harmed. *See also* **commensalism** and **mutualism**.

pathogen: The umbrella term for disease-causing organisms, including bacteria, viruses, flukes, and nematode worms, and so forth.

phagocyte: An amoeboid "eating cell" found in all types of animals that can engulf and consume other microbes.

phagocytosis: The process by which cells can engulf materials, and even other cells, by pinching off a spherical membrane-bound space called a vesicle or (if relatively large) a vacuole.

photosynthesis: The synthesis of glucose from water and carbon dioxide through the use of light energy, producing atmospheric oxygen as a byproduct. *See* **respiration**.

pica: A dietary craving for nonfood items such as chalk and dirt; sometimes a symptom of nematode infection.

plasma cell: B cell that produces large quantities of antibodies when activated. *See also* **memory cell**.

plasmid: Tiny loops of genes freely exchanged between bacteria, often bearing useful traits.

Pleistocene extinction: A highly selective extinction event about 10,000–12,000 years ago that claimed many species of megafauna, such as mammoths, mastodons, and saber-toothed cats. It may have been caused by the first organized human hunting (the overkill hypothesis).

prebiotic synthesis: The synthesis of complex organic compounds and networks of biochemical reactions prior to the origin of life.

presentation: The action of a macrophage or other antigen-presenting cell in locating and bringing a foreign antigen to the corresponding T cell for activation. *See* **cellular immune response**.

primary immune response: The cellular (presentation and activation of T cells) and humoral (B cell activation) immune responses. *See also* **cellular**

immune response, **humoral immune response**, and **secondary immune response**.

probiotic: A commercial preparation containing beneficial bacteria as a dietary supplement.

professional APC: An antigen-presenting cell that has a special type of major histocompatability complex called MHC II, which identifies traveling macrophages as messengers, not enemies.

prokaryote: A primitive cell type characteristic of bacteria and archaeans, with a cell wall and no cell nucleus or cellular organelles made from membranes (e.g., no chloroplasts or mitochondria). *See* **archaea**, **bacteria**, and **Eukarya**.

prophylactic antibiotic: Antibiotics given without a clear indication of disease as a preventative measure.

protein: A biomolecule constructed from a linear series of amino acids. Proteins provide biological structure, function, and control.

protein synthesis: The assembly of proteins from amino acids using information carried by complex forms of RNA. *See* **codon, messenger RNA (mRNA), ribosomal RNA (rRNA)**, and **transfer RNA (tRNA)**.

pus: A mixture of dead and dying neutrophils, microbes, and body cells that forms at the site of an infection.

pyrogen: A type of cytokine that triggers a rise in body temperature or fever.

realized niche (a.k.a. **actual niche**): The niche an organism occupies in the presence of competition. *See also* **fundamental niche**.

Red Queen hypothesis: Theory of biologist Leigh Van Valen that there is an upper limit to adaptation. The genetic resources of any species are finite, and because the environment never stops changing, every species will eventually exhaust its ability to adapt to those changes and will go extinct.

resistance: A physiological trait that helps prevent infection by pathogens. Although often used as synonym for immunity, resistance is a physical feature that can be directly inherited (like lacking a certain protein on the cell wall that a virus could use to enter the cell), whereas immunity is a cellular memory of a disease in the form of stored antibodies. *See also* **immunity**.

respiration: At the cellular level, the breakdown of glucose into water and carbon dioxide by using oxygen that releases stored chemical energy for use by the cell. *See* **fermentation** and **photosynthesis**.

retrovirus: A virus that uses an enzyme called reverse transcriptase to convert its RNA into DNA, which is then incorporated into the host's DNA.

reverse transcriptase: An enzyme used to turn viral RNA into DNA, which is then stitched into a host's DNA. This is the reverse of the normal process of transcription, in which the genetic message contained in a strand of DNA is copied or transcribed onto a strand of messenger RNA. The enzyme is used by viruses like HIV and feline leukemia virus. *See also* **retrovirus**.

ribosomal RNA (rRNA): A type of RNA that reads a strip of messenger RNA to allow transfer RNA to identify and fetch the next amino acid coded for. This in turn allows a ribosome to create a chain from the amino acids supplied by transfer RNA that will subsequently roll up into a functional protein. *See also* **codon**, **DNA**, and **protein synthesis**.

RNA: A single strand of nucleotides attached to a molecular backbone of sugar and phosphate molecules. The nucleotides code for synthesis of a particular protein.

RNA virus: A virus whose genetic material consists solely of RNA (not DNA). Because such viruses lack the proofreading mechanism that governs the reproduction of DNA, they mutate at a very high rate. *See* **hypermutability** and **retrovirus**.

secondary immune response: The rapid cloning of memory cells and production of appropriate antibodies in response to a second encounter with a microbe. *See* **activation, B cell, humoral immune response, primary immune response**, and **T cell**.

self-tolerance: The immune system's tolerance for the body's own cells. *See also* **autoimmune disease**.

self-reactive cell: An immune system cell that reacts to the body's own cells as if they were foreign.

stem cell: A cell produced in both embryos and adults that have the ability to differentiate into several different types of cells.

stromatolite: A thick, column-shaped mound formed by many layers of cyanobacteria biofilms; a dominant feature of Earth for 100 million years and its first true ecosystem. *See also* **oxygen revolution**.

subtype: A variant within a genus of viruses.

symbiosis: Literally, "life shared together"; a long-term biological interaction between 2 species. *See* **commensalism, mutualism**, and **parasitism**.

T cell: A lymphocyte that plays many key roles in the immune system and has a receptor on its cell surface that lets it recognize antigens bound to the major histocompatability complex. Types include cytotoxic T cells, helper T cells, and natural killer T cells. *See also* **B cell, cytotoxic cell, natural killer cell**, and **thymus**.

thermophile: A heat-loving extremophile; specifically, bacteria and archaeans that thrive in extremely hot environments like undersea thermal vents.

thymus: A gland located near the base of the neck that performs several functions in the immune system, including the filtering of mature T cells against self-reactivity. *See* **self-reactive cell**.

transfer RNA (tRNA): A form of RNA that to transfers amino acids from the cytoplasm to the ribosomes to be added to a chain of amino acids that will form a protein. It has a binding site on one end that matches up with a codon on messenger RNA and a binding site for the corresponding amino acid at the other.

vaccine: A therapeutic technique that introduces foreign antigens into an animal to help improve immune response to a particular pathogen; usually made from dead microbes, fragments of dead microbes, or microbial toxins. *See* **DNA vaccine**.

variant: A distinct genetic variant of a virus subtype.

variolation: Intentionally introducing smallpox into a human body to provide immunity. *See* **vaccine**.

vector: Any organism that carries a pathogen.

virgin soil epidemic: An epidemic in a population not previously exposed to that disease. *See* **naïve population**.

virulence: The intensity of a particular infectious disease as measured by its mortality rate.

virus: A microscopic organism consisting of a core of RNA or DNA in a protein capsule, which can only reproduce by invading a living cell and using its protein synthesis mechanisms to make and assemble copies of the virus.

weaponize: To convert or prepare a biological agent for use in warfare. *See also* **bioterrorism**.

zoonosis: A disease that pass directly from a vertebrate animal to humans and back, with no intermediate vector such as an insect.

Bibliography

Ackert, James E. "Some Influences of the American Hookworm." *American Midland Naturalist* 47, no. 3 (May 1952): 749–762. A detailed history of the Rockefeller Sanitary Commission's hookworm eradication campaign and its subsequent expansion into an international effort.

Adams, Francis V. *The Asthma Sourcebook: Everything You Need to Know.* 3rd ed. New York: McGraw-Hill, 2006. In a sea of patent medicine and self-help guides, it's nice to find a clearly written and authoritative book on the causes, symptoms, and treatments of asthma. Highly recommended for asthma sufferers and their families.

Albert, Lori J., and Robert D. Inman. "Molecular Mimicry and Autoimmunity." *New England Journal of Medicine* 341, no. 27 (December 30, 1999): 2068–2074. After absorbing the lectures on immunity and autoimmunity, you will find this seminal review of molecular mimicry in autoimmunity to be challenging but informative.

Anonymous. "M. Yersin on the Prophylaxis of Plague." *The British Medical Journal* 2, no. 2078 (Oct. 27, 1900): 1256–1257. A turn-of-the-century interview with Yersin concerning the modern outbreak of the bubonic plague and his ideas for combating it.

Appleby, Andrew B. "Epidemics and Famine in the Little Ice Age." *Journal of Interdisciplinary History* 10, no. 4 (Spring 1980): 643–663. Examines the relationship between climate, famine, and outbreaks of epidemic diseases.

Armelagos, George J. "Take Two Beers and Call Me in 1,600 Years." *Natural History* 109, no. 4 (May 2000): 50–53. A delightful article extolling the therapeutic powers of ancient Egyptian beer based on the discovery of the antibiotic tetracycline in Egyptian mummies.

Averner, M. M., and R. D. MacElroy, eds. *On the Habitability of Mars: An Approach to Planetary Ecosynthesis*. U.S. NASA SP-414, 1976. The mother lode for modern research on terraforming: a detailed NASA study of the practicality of turning Mars into a new Earth by using cyanobacteria and similar microorganisms to alter planetary conditions.

Barnaby, Wendy. *The Plague Makers: The Secret World of Biological Warfare*. New York: Continuum, 2000. A brief popular introduction to germ warfare with a survey of known national programs and lots of good information, but it suffers from sloppy editing and proofreading.

Barnett, Tony, and Alan Whiteside. *AIDS in the Twenty-First Century: Disease and Globalization*. 2nd ed. New York: Palgrave Macmillan, 2006. One of the most important books on the subject of AIDS—authoritative, comprehensive, and sobering. Considers the social and economic effects of the disease, especially in Africa, and what can be done to combat it. An invaluable reference for anyone in business or public affairs.

Barry, John M. *The Great Influenza: The Epic Story of the Deadliest Plague in History*. New York: Viking, 2004. Next to Crosby, the best general introduction to the flu. Scholarly and well written, it tells the story of the flu in part through the lives of the key researchers involved in fighting the epidemic and includes a detailed account of the origins of our modern system of medical education.

Beveridge, W. I. B. *Influenza: The Last Great Plague: An Unfinished Story of Discovery*. New York: Prodist, 1977. A good short survey of the epidemic, if a bit dated. Provides a good description of how subtypes and variant forms of the virus are formed and how they compete with one another to generate waves of fresh infection during pandemics.

Black, Francis L. "Infectious Diseases in Primitive Societies." *Science* 187, no. 4176 (February 14, 1975): 515–518. Based on an analysis of infectious diseases in isolated Amazonian tribes, Black concludes that many common infectious diseases cannot maintain themselves in small, isolated populations and were therefore not a problem for early man.

Blake, John B. "The Inoculation Controversy in Boston: 1721–1722." *The New England Quarterly* 25, no. 4 (December 1952): 489–506. A good historical account of the efforts of Cotton Mather and others to inoculate the citizens of Boston in the face of a smallpox epidemic.

Blakely, D. E. *Mass Mediated Disease: A Case Study Analysis of Three Flu Pandemics and Public Health Policy.* Lanham, MD: Lexington Books, 2006. Examines how contemporary media accounts shaped public perceptions during the pandemics of 1918 (Spanish flu), 1957 (Asian flu), and 1968 (Honk Kong flu).

Bongaarts, John, François Pelletier, and Patrick Gerland. *Poverty, Gender, and Youth: Global Trends in AIDS Mortality.* Working Paper no.16, The Population Council, 2009. One of the best sourcebooks for current information on the extent of the AIDS pandemic and its pattern of age and gender distribution. Includes a good current bibliography.

Boss, Alan. *The Crowded Universe: The Search for Living Planets.* New York: Basic Books, 2009. Takes you to the front lines of the search for life beyond the Earth; a well-written and thought-provoking introduction to astrobiology.

Brooks, F. G. "Charles Wardell Stiles." *Systematic Zoology* 13, no. 4 (Dec. 1964): 220–226. An excellent and sympathetic biography, with some entertaining detail on Stiles's childhood and school days.

———. "Charles Wardell Stiles, Intrepid Scientist." *BIOS* 18, no. 3 (Oct. 1947): 139–169. A good portrayal of the young Stiles, showing the early religious influences that were to motivate him during the hookworm campaign, such as the gift for language he acquired from translating the Bible, which in turn allowed him to study in Germany and at the Pasteur Institute.

Brown, E. Richard. *Rockefeller Medicine Men: Medicine and Capitalism in America.* Berkeley: University of California Press, 1979. Takes the contrary view to Ettling's thesis in *The Germ of Laziness*, claiming that the driving forces behind the hookworm campaign were more political and economic than social and philanthropic.

Bud, Robert. *Penicillin: Triumph and Tragedy*. New York: Oxford University Press, 2007. A well-written and authoritative history of the discovery, application, and importance of penicillin and the evolution of resistant microbes.

Burney, D. A., and T. F. Flannery. "Fifty Millennia of Catastrophic Extinctions after Human Contact." *Trends in Ecology & Evolution* 20, no. 7 (July 2005): 395–401. Reviews the various theories proposed to explain the Pleistocene extinction event and concludes that we need to have a deeper appreciation of the way humans affect ecosystems.

Bushnell, O. A. *The Gifts of Civilization: Germs and Genocide in Hawaii*. Honolulu: University of Hawaii Press, 1993. Examines the effect of Captain Cook and other European explorers and exploiters on the health and abundance of native Hawaiians, with an excellent bibliography.

Byerly, C. R. *Fever of War: The Influenza Epidemic in the U.S. Army During World War I*. New York: New York University Press, 2005. A scholarly and in-depth account of the effects of the flu both in military camps and on the front, as well as the conflicting roles of medical doctors in wartime. Argues that the war created the pandemic by giving the virus a new environment in which to mutate and thrive.

Cassedy, James H. "The Germ of Laziness in the South, 1900–1915: Charles Wardell Stiles and the Progressive Paradox." *Bulletin of the History of Medicine* 45 (1971): 159–169. Discusses the contrast between economic and evangelical motives in the Rockefeller Sanitary Commission's campaign to eradicate hookworm disease.

Clark, Thomas Dionysius. *The Emerging South*. 2d ed. New York: Oxford University Press, 1968. A classic study of the rise of the New South; dated but still relevant.

Clark, William R. *In Defense of Self: How the Immune System Really Works*. New York: Oxford University Press, 2008. An excellent and very readable introduction to the bewildering complexities of the immune system. Highly recommended.

Cohn, Samuel Kline. *The Black Death Transformed: Disease and Culture in Early Renaissance Europe.* New York: Arnold/Oxford University Press, 2002. Takes the controversial view that the Black Death and the bubonic plague are actually different diseases with distinct differences in their virulence and epidemiology.

Cole, Leonard A. *Clouds of Secrecy: The Army's Germ Warfare Tests over Populated Areas.* Totowa, NJ: Rowman & Littlefield, 1999. A shocking exposé of the secret germ warfare experiments conducted in San Francisco, the New York City subway system, and elsewhere, including a detailed account of the lawsuit by Edward Nevin over the death of his grandfather, the first official victim of U. S. germ warfare.

Cooper, Henry S. F. *The Search for Life on Mars: Evolution of an Idea.* New York: Holt, Rinehart and Winston, 1980. A good contemporary account of NASA's quest to find life on Mars, with much insider historical information. Not in print, but regularly available through Amazon.

Cowdrey, Albert E. *This Land, this South: An Environmental History.* New Perspectives on the South. Lexington: University Press of Kentucky, 1983. An excellent and classic survey of the ways that Southern culture and history have been shaped by environment.

Crawford, Dorothy. *The Invisible Enemy: A Natural History of Viruses.* New York: Oxford University Press, 2000. A well-written introduction to the world of viruses, including an extensive discussion of viruses and cancer.

Crawford, Dorothy H. *Deadly Companions: How Microbes Shaped Our History.* New York: Oxford University Press, 2007. One of the best books in print on the coevolution of humans and microbes; well-written, absorbing, and informative, with an excellent bibliography and glossary.

Crosby, Alfred W. *America's Forgotten Pandemic: The Influenza of 1918.* 2nd ed. New York: Cambridge University Press, 2003. Crosby is one of the most authoritative sources on the flu, and his book is an excellent starting point for further research. Previously published as *Epidemic and Peace, 1918* (1976).

———. *The Columbian Exchange: Biological and Cultural Consequences of 1492*. Contributions in American Studies. Vol. 2. Westport, CT.: Greenwood, 1972. One of the most significant scholarly studies of the great exchange of culture, trade goods, crops, livestock, and diseases from the Old World to the New in the wake of the voyage of Columbus.

Davey, Basiro, Tim Halliday, and Mark Hirst. *Human Biology and Health: An Evolutionary Approach*. Health and Disease Series. 3d ed. Philadelphia, PA: Open University, 2001. An excellent general textbook of evolutionary medicine, including several chapters covering basic biology and evolutionary theory.

Davidson, Elizabeth W. *Big Fleas Have Little Fleas: How Discoveries of Invertebrate Diseases Are Advancing Modern Science*. Tucson: University of Arizona Press, 2006. Surveys the many ways in which microbes, parasitic worms, and the biological controls derived from them are being used for our benefit.

Davies, Paul. *The Fifth Miracle: The Search for the Origin and Meaning of Life*. New York: Simon and Schuster, 2000. Davies brings his usual skill at communicating science to nonscientists to the challenging topic of where and how life began, including extremophiles, life on Mars, and the theory of panspermia.

Davis, Joel. *Defending the Body: Unraveling the Mysteries of Immunology*. New York: Atheneum, 1989. A general introduction to immunity for the nonscientist, with a particularly good section on AIDS; unusual for its scientist-oriented journalistic style, which brings the reader into the front lines of immunological research.

Dawson, A. "Hannibal and Chemical Warfare." *The Classical Journal* 63, no. 3 (Dec. 1967): 117–125. Explores the possibility that Hannibal, the great Carthaginian general and enemy of the Romans, may have used chemical weapons.

De Kruif, Paul. *Microbe Hunters*. New York: Harcourt, Brace and Company, 1926. A classic, still in print after nearly 85 years, with detailed and highly personal biographies of 12 great men who dedicated their lives to unraveling the mysteries of the microscopic world. Highly recommended.

Defoe, Daniel. *Journal of the Plague Year*. Oxford World Classics. Oxford: Oxford University Press, 2010. The classic contemporary account of the Black Death's rampage though 17th-century London.

Des Marais, D. J., and M. R. Walter. "Astrobiology: Exploring the Origins, Evolution, and Distribution of Life in the Universe." *Annual Review of Ecology and Systematics* 30 (1999): 397–420. An excellent literature review of the field of astrobiology, also called exobiology or xenobiology, with a good assessment of primary hypotheses and discoveries on the origin of life and the possibility of life in outer space.

Despommier, Dickson D. *West Nile Story*. New York: Apple Trees Productions, 2001. Describes the search for the West Nile virus in New York City at the turn of the century, weaving together the roles of biology, politics, and human behavior in the spread of emergent diseases.

Diamond, Jared M. *Guns, Germs, and Steel: The Fates of Human Societies*. New York: Norton, 2005. A modern classic, tracing the rise and dispersal of the human race and the often subtle relationships between geography and human culture and history. Includes a good account of the relationship between livestock diseases and the great Columbian Exchange.

Dobson, Mary. *Disease: The Extraordinary Stories Behind History's Deadliest Killers*. London: Quercus, 2007. As a former college librarian, I'm always reluctant to recommend anything remotely resembling a coffee-table book, but Dobson knows her stuff, and the engaging and informative style and superb illustrations put this one in the winner's circle. Includes a detailed timeline. A word of warning, some of you might find the cover a bit unsettling.

Dobyns, Henry F., and William R. Swagerty. *Their Number Become Thinned*. Native American Historic Demography Series. Knoxville, TN: University of Tennessee Press/ Newberry Library Center for the History of the American Indian, 1983. An excellent review of the size and distribution of precolonial

Native American populations and the effects of diseases and other factors in reducing them.

Duckett, Serge. "Ernest Duchesne and the Concept of Fungal Antibiotic Therapy." *The Lancet* 354, no. 9195 (1999): 2068–2071. A good biographical sketch of Duchesne, focused on his discovery of the antibiotic properties of penicillin and his pioneering recognition of the importance of microbial competition.

Duncan, Kirsty. *Hunting the 1918 Flu: One Scientist's Search for a Killer Virus*. Toronto: University of Toronto Press, 2003. Chronicles the efforts of amateur virologist Kirsty Duncan to recover an intact sample of the 1918 virus.

Elkin, W. B. "An Inquiry into the Causes of the Decrease of the Hawaiian People." *The American Journal of Sociology* 8, no. 3 (November 1902): 398–411. A valuable turn-of-the-century survey of the gradual destruction of Hawaiian native populations, including a discussion of the effects of epidemic diseases.

Eppig, Christopher, Corey L. Fincher, and Randy Thornhill. "Parasite Prevalence and the Worldwide Distribution of Cognitive Ability." *Proceedings of the Royal Society B* 277, no. 1701 (2010): 3801–3808. The latest study of the effects of disease on regional intelligence, which finds a very high correlation between national IQ levels and the extent of infectious diseases.

Epstein, Helen. *The Invisible Cure: Africa, the West, and the Fight against AIDS*. New York: Farrar, Straus and Giroux, 2007. An important book on the AIDS crisis, suggesting that Western efforts to fight AIDS in Africa might be counterproductive and that the problem might be better handled from an African perspective. Examines the changes in sexual behavior behind sharp declines in AIDS in Uganda and Tanzania.

Ettling, John. *The Germ of Laziness: Rockefeller Philanthropy and Public Health in the New South*. Cambridge, MA: Harvard University Press, 1981. The best book available about the commission's efforts to eradicate hookworm in the South. In contrast to other authorities, Ettling takes the view that Stiles's motivation was more evangelical than economic.

Ewald, Paul W. *Evolution of Infectious Disease.* New York: Oxford University Press, 1994. A solid introduction to evolutionary medicine from one of its founders; very accessible to the nonscientist, with a particular emphasis on the evolution of virulence. Includes an extensive bibliography.

————. *Plague Time: The New Germ Theory of Disease.* New York: Anchor Books, 2002. A controversial book in which Ewald proposes that many modern ailments, like heart disease and Alzheimer's, may actually be due to chronic infectious diseases.

Fagan, Brian M. *The Little Ice Age: How Climate Made History, 1300–1850.* New York: Basic Books, 2000. A pioneering work on the effects of climate on human history, detailing the harsh weather that led to widespread famine, poor health, and increased vulnerability to diseases like the Black Death.

Fehervari, Zoltan, and Shimon Sakaguchi. "Peacekeepers of the Immune System." *Scientific American* 295, no. 4 (Oct. 2006): 56–63. A readable account of the recent discovery of a subpopulation of helper T cells called regulatory T cells and their possible use in fighting autoimmune diseases and cancer.

Fenn, Elizabeth A. "Biological Warfare in Eighteenth-Century North America: Beyond Jeffery Amherst." *The Journal of American History* 86, no. 4 (March 2000): 1552–1580. Reviews the use of smallpox by colonial officials against tribes of Native Americans, presenting convincing evidence that such tactics were actually employed.

Finlay, B. B. "The Art of Bacterial Warfare." *Scientific American* 302, no. 2 (2010): 56–63. Looks at the way bacteria can hijack cellular mechanisms and cellular communication for their own benefit through bacterial behaviors and bacterial toxins and discusses strategies used by *Escherichia coli* and *Salmonella*.

Garrett, Laurie. *The Coming Plague: Newly Emerging Diseases in a World Out of Balance.* New York: Farrar, Straus and Giroux, 1994. A somewhat sensational and ominous look at the future of emergent diseases as microbes find ways to adapt to the new evolutionary opportunities provided by new technology.

Gluckman, Peter, Alan Beedle, and Mark Hanson. *Principles of Evolutionary Medicine.* Oxford: Oxford University Press, 2009. An excellent and authoritative text covering the basic biology behind human diseases, microbial and otherwise, including the fundamentals of variation, natural selection, and life-history strategies. Challenging in parts, but accessible to the nonscientist.

Gottfried, Robert Steven. *The Black Death: Natural and Human Disaster in Medieval Europe.* New York: Free Press, 1983. A well-written survey of the progress of the 14th century pandemic, with a good summary of its social, political, and historical effects on the medieval world.

Gronlund, Hans, Tiiu Saarne, Guro Gafvelin, and Marianne van Hage. "The Major Cat Allergen, Fel d 1, in Diagnosis and Therapy." *International Archives of Allergy and Immunology* 151, no. 4 (2010): 265–274. For those who suffer from cat allergies, some solid scientific discussion of the problem, with an excellent bibliography. Be prepared to do a lot of skimming if you're not an immunologist!

Gross, Ludwik. "How the Plague Bacillus and Its Transmission through Fleas Were Discovered: Reminiscences from My Years at the Pasteur Institute in Paris." *Proceedings of the National Academy of Sciences of the United States of America* 92, no. 17 (August 15, 1995): 7609–7611. An excellent account of the pioneering work of Yersin and Simond in the third plague pandemic.

Haensch, Stephanie, Raffaella Bianucci, Michel Signoli, Minoarisoa Rajerison, et al. "Distinct Clones of *Yersinia pestis* Caused the Black Death." *PLOS Pathogens* 6, no. 10 (October 2010): 1–8. DNA analysis of the remains of medieval plague victims from mass graves across Europe confirm that the Black Death was actually caused by *Yersinia pestis.*

Harper, David R., and Andrea S. Meyer. *Of Mice, Men, and Microbes: Hantavirus*. San Diego: Academic Press, 1999. A comprehensive study of the emergence of hantavirus among the Navajo and the evolutionary response of microbes to natural environmental changes.

Harris, Sheldon H. *Factories of Death: Japanese Biological Warfare 1932–45 and the American Cover-Up*. New York: Routledge, 1994. An eye-opening account of the secret Japanese warfare campaign against China and America by the maddest of mad scientists, Shiro Ishii, and the subsequent cover-up by the Allies. Extensively researched and referenced; out of print but regularly available through Amazon.

Henderson, Donald A. *Smallpox: The Death of a Disease: The Inside Story of Eradicating a Worldwide Killer*. Amherst, NY: Prometheus Books, 2009. An excellent and detailed review of the global campaign to eliminate smallpox from the planet, including a good short history of the disease.

Herring, Ann, and Alan C. Swedlund. *Plagues and Epidemics: Infected Spaces Past and Present*. Wenner-Gren International Symposium Series. English ed. New York: Berg, 2010. A good collection of current scholarly articles on several epidemic diseases, both historical and modern.

Honigsbaum, M. *Living With Enza: The Forgotten Story of Britain and the Great Flu Pandemic of 1918*. London: Macmillan, 2009. A detailed and scholarly account of the British experience during the pandemic. Later chapters provide a good summary of more recent encounters with the flu and efforts to sequence the 1918 virus.

Hopkins, Donald R. *Princes and Peasants: Smallpox in History*. Chicago: University of Chicago Press, 1983. An excellent survey of smallpox in human history, from ancient Egypt to the modern-day campaign to eradicate the disease. One of the best scholarly books on smallpox, with an extensive bibliography.

Hotez, Peter J., Jeffrey M. Bethony, David J. Diemert, Mark Pearson, and Alex Loukas. "Developing Vaccines to Combat Hookworm Infection and Intestinal Schistosomiasis." *Nature Reviews: Microbiology* 8 (November

2010): 814–826. A good recent review of the global status of hookworm and schistosomiasis, with a detailed discussion of available therapies. A bit technical in parts, but readable, with good illustrations and a very extensive bibliography.

Hotez, Peter J., Paul J. Brindley, Jeffrey M. Bethony, Charles H. King, Edward J. Pearce, and Julie Jacobson. "Helminth Infections: The Great Neglected Tropical Diseases." *The Journal of Clinical Investigation* 118, no. 4 (April 2008): 1311–1321. A good review of the current state of research on parasitic worm infections, their global extent, and our responsibility for taking international action to control the problem.

Hoyle, Fred, and N. C. Wickramasinghe. *Diseases from Space*. London: Dent, 1979. A very controversial book in which the authors extend the theory of panspermia to propose that emerging diseases might have an extraterrestrial origin.

———. *Living Comets*. Cardiff, UK: University College Cardiff Press, 1985. Proposes that interstellar microbes, trapped in cometary dust, are carried to Earth during the passage of comets.

Jackson, Mark. *Allergy: The History of a Modern Malady*. London: Reaktion, 2006. A good review of the history of allergy, starting with the work of Pirquet and continuing to the latest modern research. Highly recommended for allergy sufferers.

Jeans, Roger B., Jr. "Alarm in Washington: A Wartime 'Exposé' of Japan's Biological Warfare Program." *The Journal of Military History* 71, no. 2 (Apr. 2007): 411–439. Looks at media and government reaction to a badly written book titled *Japan's Secret Weapon*, an early work on Japanese biowarfare, which drew attention to a sensitive area the federal government did not want the press or public to examine.

Jones, E. W. *Influenza 1918: Diseases, Death, and Struggle in Winnipeg*. Toronto, ON: University of Toronto Press, 2007. Uses Winnipeg's encounter with the 1918 Flu as a case study in the roles of social institutions and public health policies in pandemics. Concludes that the flu had a more severe impact on the poor, the working class, and women than is generally acknowledged.

Karlen, Arno. *Biography of a Germ*. New York: Pantheon Books, 2000. A good popular account of the emergence, biology, and ecology of Lyme disease.

————. *Man and Microbes: Disease and Plagues in History and Modern Times*. New York: Simon & Schuster, 1996. Traces the history of our coevolution with epidemic diseases, including the rise of crowd diseases and the modern emergence of new diseases related to our continuing cultural and technological development. Includes an excellent bibliography.

Kelly, John. *The Great Mortality: An Intimate History of the Black Death, the Most Devastating Plague of All Time*. New York: HarperCollins Publishers, 2005. A popular and fast-paced account of the plague in the 14th century. Kelly does a good job of bringing the medieval world alive but sometimes takes a few historic liberties in trying to make us feel the personal impact of the plague.

Knollenberg, Bernhard. "General Amherst and Germ Warfare." *The Mississippi Valley Historical Review* 41, no. 3 (Dec. 1954): 489–494. Presents contemporary letters and notes to determine whether the military used smallpox as a biological weapon during the Pontiac Indian Rebellion, concluding that although someone deliberately gave blankets infected with smallpox to Indian diplomatic representatives, there is no direct evidence that they were instructed to do so by their superiors.

Koblentz, Gregory. "Pathogens as Weapons: The International Security Implications of Biological Warfare." *International Security* 28, no. 3 (Winter 2003): 84–122. Reviews the characteristics of pathogens used as weapons and how to defend against them, concluding that the intense secrecy surrounding their use is a destabilizing factor in bioweapons security.

Koenig, Robert L. *The Fourth Horseman: One Man's Secret Mission to Wage the Great War in America*. New York: PublicAffairs, 2006. The tangled tale of Anton Dilger, the son of an American war hero who grew up to run a secret German biological warfare lab in the suburbs of Washington DC during World War I.

Kolata, Gina Bari. *Flu: The Story of the Great Influenza Pandemic of 1918 and the Search for the Virus That Caused It*. New York: Farrar, Straus and Giroux, 1999. A good popular introduction to the pandemic, with a lengthy account of the subsequent search for an intact virus.

Koplow, David A. *Smallpox: The Fight to Eradicate a Global Scourge*. Berkeley: University of California Press, 2003. Traces the history of the global campaign to eradicate smallpox, including chapters on the biology of the virus, its use as a biological weapon, and the morality of driving it into extinction.

Kotb, Malak, John D. Fraser, and the American Society for Microbiology. *Superantigens: Molecular Basis for Their Role in Human Diseases*. Washington, DC: ASM Press, 2007. A current collection of scientific papers on the role of superantigens in human diseases, including state-of-the-art therapeutic techniques. Very challenging, like most primary literature in this field.

Krohn, Katherine E., Bob Hall, Keith Williams, and Charles Barnett III. *The 1918 Flu Pandemic*. Mankato, MN: Capstone Press, 2008. A graphic novel depicting the pandemic in comic format. Valuable for educators.

Lagerkvist, Ulf. *Pioneers of Microbiology and the Nobel Prize*. River Edge, NJ: World Scientific, 2003. Biographies of some of the great pioneers of immunology and microbiology: Paul Ehrlich, Emil von Behring, Robert Koch, and Elie Metchnikoff.

Lappé, Marc. *Evolutionary Medicine: Rethinking the Origins of Disease*. San Francisco: Sierra Club Books, 1994. An excellent introduction to evolutionary medicine. Concludes that considering traditional medical problems from the standpoint of ecological and evolutionary theory may offer new solutions to old diseases.

Bibliography

Lau, S., and P. M. Matricardi. "Worms, Asthma, and the Hygiene Hypothesis." *Lancet* 367, no. 9522 (May 13, 2006): 1556–1558. A short but informative review of the hygiene hypothesis concerning asthma and exposure to parasitic worms, with a good bibliography.

Leskowitz, Sidney. "Immunologic Tolerance." *Bioscience* 18, no. 11 (Nov. 1968): 1030–1034, 1039. May be a little challenging for the general reader but provides a concise review of the biology of tolerance and antigen structure and the theoretical issues remaining to be resolved in this important area of immunology.

Levenson, Jacob. *The Secret Epidemic: The Story of AIDS and Black America.* New York: Pantheon Books, 2004. An eloquent and absorbing account of the way AIDS affects the lives of individuals; one of the most heartfelt and best-written books on the subject of AIDS.

Levy, Buddy. *Conquistador: Hernán Cortés, King Montezuma, and the Last Stand of the Aztecs.* New York: Bantam Books, 2008. A highly detailed and scholarly study that reads like a novel, discussing the many military, political, and biological factors (like smallpox) that led to the downfall of the Aztecs.

Link, William A. "Privies, Progressivism, and Public Schools: Health Reform and Education in the Rural South, 1909–1920." *The Journal of Southern History* 54, no. 4 (November 1988): 623–642. Reviews the effects of the Rockefeller Sanitary Commission hookworm program on student health, school attendance, and academic performance, concluding that the commission had a significant and continuing positive effect on local and regional education, such as regular medical examination of school children.

Macfarlane, Gwyn. *Alexander Fleming, the Man and the Myth.* Cambridge, MA: Harvard University Press, 1984. Good biography of the great medical pioneer; addresses the controversy over the shared credit between Fleming and his less-recognized colleagues and concludes that Fleming himself was not after personal glory for their shared discovery.

Mak, Tak W., and Mary E. Saunders. *Primer to the Immune Response*. Boston: Academic Press/Elsevier, 2008. A good general textbook on immunity, profusely illustrated and relatively well written. The word "primer" in the title may be a misnomer, but it does make you wonder how much more formidable an advanced textbook would be!

Mangold, Tom, and Jeff Goldberg. *Plague Wars: A True Story of Biological Warfare*. New York: St. Martin's Press, 2000. A highly detailed and chilling history of biological warfare programs in Russia, Iraq, and South Africa, with an emphasis on the Russian program.

Margulis, Lynn, and Dorion Sagan. *Microcosmos: Four Billion Years of Microbial Evolution*. Berkeley: University of California Press, 1997. Margulis is a towering figure in biodiversity and a skilled writer. The book highlights the many contributions microbes have made to the history of life and the evolution of the modern world.

Martin, Paul S. *Twilight of the Mammoths: Ice Age Extinctions and the Rewilding of America*. Organisms and Environments. Vol. 8. Berkeley: University of California Press, 2005. A scholarly yet readable investigation of the role of human hunters in the Pleistocene extinction event.

Mayor, Adrienne. *Greek Fire, Poison Arrows, and Scorpion Bombs: Biological and Chemical Warfare in the Ancient World*. Woodstock, NY: Overlook Press, 2003. A well-written and absorbing history of germ warfare in the ancient world, highly recommended. Warning—this book can be hard to put down!

McNeill, William Hardy. *Plagues and Peoples*. Garden City, NY: Anchor Press, 1976. One of the best books ever written on the coevolution of the human race with its microbial adversaries, including the social, political, and ecological context of epidemic diseases. Highly recommended.

Merrell, D. S., and S. Falkow. "Frontal and Stealth Attack Strategies in Microbial Pathogenesis." *Nature* 430, no. 6996 (Jul. 8, 2004): 250–256. An excellent but advanced overview of microbial strategies, both direct and stealthy, with the focus on molecular-level immune system mechanisms.

Moote, A. Lloyd, and Dorothy C. Moote. *The Great Plague: The Story of London's Most Deadly Year*. Baltimore, MD: Johns Hopkins University Press, 2004. A good detailed account of the Great Plague of London; scholarly and thorough, yet told from the viewpoint of the people who suffered through it.

Morens, David M., and Anthony S. Fauci. "The 1918 Influenza Pandemic: Insights for the 21st Century." *Journal of Infectious Diseases* 195, no. 7 (April 1, 2007): 1018–1028. Considers the origins of the virus and its age-related pattern of mortality, including a table summarizing current information on basic questions posed by the pandemic.

Morse, Stephen S. *Emerging Viruses*. New York: Oxford University Press, 1993. A collection of authoritative and scholarly articles on the modern emergence of infectious diseases like AIDS, Ebola, and Hantaan fever.

Mullen, T. *The Last Town on Earth*. New York: Random House, 2006. A rare novel about the flu that tells the story of a young soldier who talks his way through a quarantine roadblock in a small mining town in Washington, triggering a series of events that illustrates the problems faced by small communities during the pandemic.

Nesse, Randolph M., and George C. Williams. *Why We Get Sick: The New Science of Darwinian Medicine*. New York: Vintage Books, 1996. A great introduction to the coevolution of humans with their microbial pathogens. Includes material on the evolutionary arms race, microbial strategies, and allergies as well as a survey of nonmicrobial disease problems related to the nature of human evolution and lifestyles (evolutionary legacies and diseases of civilization).

Nuland, Sherwin B. *The Doctors' Plague: Germs, Childbed Fever, and the Strange Story of Ignaz Semmelweis*. Great Discoveries. New York: W. W. Norton, 2003. An engaging biography of the doctor who taught us to wash our hands—a troubled man with a noble but elusive goal.

Oro, J., Stanley L. Miller, and Antonio Lazcano. "The Origin and Early Evolution of Life on Earth." *Annual Review of Earth and Planetary Sciences* 18 (1990): 317–356. An excellent, if challenging, review of experiments in prebiotic synthesis and the origin of life, with an inside perspective from Stanley Miller.

Patterson, Andrea. "Germs and Jim Crow: The Impact of Microbiology on Public Health Policies in Progressive Era American South." *Journal of the History of Biology* 42, no. 3 (Fall 2009): 529–559. Addresses the racial attitudes that excluded African Americans from public health programs and how these attitudes were exploited by the eugenics movement and other racist organizations. Well written, well researched, and very disturbing.

Pettit, Dorothy Ann, and Janice Bailie. *A Cruel Wind: Pandemic Flu in America, 1918–1920.* Murfreesboro, TN: Timberlane Books, 2008. An excellent introduction to the pandemic; stands with Barry and Crosby as one of the best books on the flu. Scholarly and well-written, it tells the story of the flu through contemporary accounts, with an emphasis on the individuals who struggled against it.

Pier, Gerald Bryan, Jeffrey B. Lyczak, and Lee M. Wetzler. *Immunology, Infection, and Immunity.* Washington, DC: ASM Press, 2004. If textbooks were worth their weight in gold, anyone possessing this book would be very wealthy indeed! A good introduction to an extremely complex subject at an advanced undergraduate or medical-school level.

Playfair, J. H. L. *Living with Germs.* New York: Oxford University Press, 2004. A good, concise introduction to the immune system for nonscientists.

Porter, K. A. "Pale Horse, Pale Rider." *The Collected Short Stories of Katherine Anne Porter.* Orlando: Harcourt Books, 1979. The only major work of fiction on the flu. Porter and her fiancé both fell ill, but only she survived the pandemic.

Preston, Richard. *The Hot Zone.* New York: Random House, 1994. A chilling account of the emergence of Ebola and its near escape into Washington DC.

Purkitt, Helen E., and Stephen Burgess. "South Africa's Chemical and Biological Warfare Programme: A Historical and International Perspective." *Journal of Southern African Studies* 28, no. 2 (Jun. 2002): 229–253. A detailed analysis of one of the planet's best-kept secrets, the extensive germ warfare program developed by South Africa.

Ramenofsky, Ann F. *Vectors of Death: The Archaeology of European Contact.* Albuquerque: University of New Mexico Press, 1987. An independent and scholarly effort to chart the size of native populations and determine the effect of European contact in the 16th century.

Reidel, Stefan. "Biological Warfare and Bioterrorism: A Historical Review." *Baylor Univeristy Medical Center Proceedings* 17 (2004): 400–406. Hard to locate but worth the effort, this is a concise review of the history of biological warfare with a lengthy bibliography.

Reisman, Robert E. "Insect Stings." *New England Journal of Medicine* 331, no. 8 (1994): 523–527. An excellent review of allergic responses to insect stings; an important source for those with severe bee and insect allergies.

Ripple, William J., and Blaire Van Valkenburgh. "Linking Top-Down Forces to the Pleistocene Megafaunal Extinctions." *Bioscience* 60, no. 7 (July–August 2010): 516–526. Reviews evidence that human hunting caused the Pleistocene extinctions and concludes that the vanished species were especially vulnerable due to their low population densities and their susceptibility to predators.

Rockefeller Sanitary Commission for the Eradication of Hookworm Disease. *Publication.* No. 1–9. Washington, DC: Office of the Commission, 1910–1915. A very thick stack of government documents detailing the long and thorough investigation of the commission over several years and several states.

Sachs, Jessica Snyder. *Good Germs, Bad Germs: Health and Survival in a Bacterial World*. New York: Hill and Wang, 2007. A well written survey of how microbes affect our lives, with a particularly useful section on the relationship between hygiene and immunity. Includes several examples of how microbes can be used to improve our health and welfare.

Sompayrac, Lauren. *How the Immune System Works*. 3rd ed. Malden, MA: Blackwell, 2008. A popular, concise guide to the bewildering complexity of the immune system that has saved the skin of many a medical student cramming for exams; clearly written, well organized, and profusely illustrated.

Sartin, Jeffrey S. "Infectious Diseases during the Civil War: The Triumph of the 'Third Army.'" *Clinical Infectious Diseases* 16, no. 4 (April 1993): 580–584. An informative summary of the extent of disease-related casualties, versus combat casualties, in the American Civil War, concluding that 2/3 of the total casualties were due to disease.

Savitt, Todd Lee, and James Harvey Young. *Disease and Distinctiveness in the American South*. Knoxville: University of Tennessee Press, 1988. A collection of papers on the effects of various epidemic diseases on Southern health and history, including an informative essay on hookworm.

Scientific American. *Infectious Disease: A Scientific American Reader*. Chicago: University of Chicago Press, 2008. A collection of 30 articles published in Scientific American between 1993 and 2007 on viruses, bacteria, and other microbial pathogens, including several articles on immunity.

Scott, Susan, and C. J. Duncan. *Return of the Black Death*. Hoboken, NJ: Wiley, 2004. A good treatment of the medieval and modern outbreaks of the plague, maintaining that the 2 pandemics were caused by 2 different diseases, with the Black Death caused by an unknown Ebola-like virus.

Sencer, D. J., and J. D. Millar. "Reflections on the 1976 Swine Flu Vaccination Program." *Emerging Infectious Diseases* 12, no. 1 (January 2006): 29–33. A good review of the policy decisions surrounding the swine flu vaccination program, with lessons learned for coping with future epidemics of avian flu.

Shilts, Randy. *And the Band Played On: Politics, People, and the AIDS Epidemic*. Rev. ed. New York: St. Martin's Griffin, 2007. An important and controversial work first published in 1987 and recently revised and reprinted. Shilts followed the first 5 years of the AIDS epidemic as a reporter for the San Fancisco Chronicle and deplored the inaction and grandstanding he observed on all sides of the issue.

Silverstein, A. M. "Autoimmunity versus Horror Autotoxicus: The Struggle for Recognition." *Nature Immunology* 2, no. 4 (April 2001): 279–281. Studies the early history of immunology, noting the negative effects of Paul Ehrlich's theories on the acknowledgement of the existence and prevalence of autoimmune diseases.

———. "Clemens Freiherr von Pirquet: Explaining Immune Complex Disease in 1906." *Nature Immunology* 1, no. 6 (December 2000): 453–455. A good sketch of von Pirquet's career, including his famous research in fungal antibiotics.

Smith, Geddes. *Plague on Us*. New York: The Commonwealth Fund, 1941. A classic work on the epidemiology of infectious diseases; dated but informative and well written.

Spellberg, Brad. *Rising Plague: The Global Threat from Deadly Bacteria and Our Dwindling Arsenal to Fight Them*. New York: Prometheus Books, 2009. A compelling review of the rise of antibiotic resistance and a critique of the current state of drug research, or lack thereof, with several suggestions for restoring the balance.

Stiles, Charles Wardell. "Hookworm Disease in its Relation to the Negro." *Public Health Reports (1896–1970)* 24, no. 31 (Jul. 30, 1909): 1083–1089. Stiles acknowledges the Rockefeller Sanitary Commission's neglect of the problem of hookworms in Southern black communities but concludes that exposure in Africa has kept them relatively immune to its effects.

Suttle, C. A. "Viruses in the Sea." *Nature* 437, no. 7057 (September 15, 2005): 356–361. A detailed look at the vast diversity and staggering abundance of viruses in the ocean that discusses aquatic viruses as a possible source of emerging terrestrial diseases.

Taubenberger, J. K., and D. M. Morens. "1918 Influenza: The Mother of all Pandemics." *Emerging Infectious Diseases* 12, no. 1 (January 2006): 15–22. Examines the origins and epidemiological patterns of the 1918 Flu, the reasons for its high virulence, and the causes of the W-shaped age-distribution curve of flu mortality.

Taubenberger, Jeffery K., Johan V. Hultin, and David M. Morens. "Discovery and Characterization of the 1918 Pandemic Influenza Virus in Historical Context." *Antiviral Therapy* 12, no. 4 (2007): 581–591. A thorough review of the history of efforts to identify the biological nature of the 1918 Flu leading to the modern sequencing of the viral genome.

Tauber, A. I. "Metchnikoff and the Phagocytosis Theory." *Nature Reviews Molecular Cell Biology* 4, no. 11 (November 2003): 897–901. Puts Metchnikoff's work on immunity in the larger context of the contemporary theoretical issues in general biology that he was interested in solving.

Tuchman, Barbara Wertheim. *A Distant Mirror: The Calamitous 14ᵗʰ Century*. New York: Knopf, 1984. A classic and absorbing account of a period the author claims was one of the worst times to be alive in human history, an age marked by a series of unfortunate events, including the beginning of the Little Ice Age and the onset of the Black Death.

U. S. Army Medical Department, Borden Institute. *Medical Aspects of Chemical and Biological Warfare*. http://www.bordeninstitute.army.mil/published_volumes/chemBio/chembio.html. An exhaustive and authoritative online textbook of chemical and biological warfare, with individual chapters devoted to plague, anthrax, smallpox and other perennial favorites. Chapters are available in PDF format.

Waller, John. *The Discovery of the Germ: Twenty Years that Transformed the Way We Think about Disease*. Revolutions in Science. New York: Columbia

University Press, 2002. A brief but fascinating survey of the most critical period in the formulation of germ theory. Very highly recommended.

Walters, Mark Jerome. *Six Modern Plagues and How We Are Causing Them.* Washington, DC: Island Press/Shearwater Books, 2003. A good survey of modern diseases caused by humans' impact on natural environments, including mad cow disease, AIDS, salmonella DT-104, Lyme disease, hantavirus, and West Nile virus.

Ward, Peter Douglas, and Donald Brownlee. *Rare Earth: Why Complex Life is Uncommon in the Universe.* New York: Copernicus, 2000. Takes the view that complex alien life forms may actually be scarcer than we think due to a variety of geological, physical, and biological factors illustrated by the history of our own planet. Microbial life, however, may be abundant in the cosmos.

Watkins, Renee Neu. "Petrarch and the Black Death: From Fear to Monuments." *Studies in the Renaissance* 19 (1972): 196–223. A scholarly study of Petrarch's reaction to the outbreak of Black Death that claimed his lover Laura and most of his friends, as well as its effects on his writing. Conveys the despair of the plague's survivors.

Watkins, W. E., and E. Pollitt. "'Stupidity or Worms': Do Intestinal Worms Impair Mental Performance?" *Psychological Bulletin* 121, no. 2 (Mar. 1997): 171–191. Reviews 80 years of research on the cognitive effects of parasitic worm infection and concludes that the effect is significant but that not all victims recover cognitive performance after treatment.

Westing, Arthur H. "The Threat of Biological Warfare." *Bioscience* 35, no. 10 (November 1985): 627–633. A good article for the general reader on the spread of biological weapons and the possibility of a biological arms race with the Russians.

Wilcox, Lynne S. "Worms and Germs, Drink and Dementia: US Health, Society, and Policy in the Early 20th Century." *Preventing Chronic Disease: Public Health Research, Practice, and Policy* 5, no.4 (October 2008): 1–12. Examines hookworm, pellagra, alcoholism, and cholera to show how public policy is often shaped by social and political forces instead of by logic and scientific data.

Woese, Carl R., Otto Kandler, and Mark L. Wheelis. "Towards a Natural System of Organisms: Proposal for the Domains Archaea, Bacteria, and Eucarya." *Proceedings of the National Academy of Sciences of the United States of America* 87, no. 12 (Jun. 1990): 4576–4579. The classic paper in which Carl Woese formally defined and named the Domain Archaea and proposed the 3-domain system, one of the most significant publications in biodiversity in the last 50 years.

Wolfe, Thomas. *Look Homeward Angel.* New York: Scribner, 1929. Hailed by many as the "great American novel," Wolfe's autobiographical masterpiece is one of the few works of fiction that mentions the flu. His sad and eloquent description of his brother Ben on his deathbed is a scene that was repeated hundreds of thousands of times across America during the 1918 pandemic.

Wray, Matt. *Not Quite White: White Trash and the Boundaries of Whiteness.* Durham, NC: Duke University Press, 2006. A fascinating scholarly study of the phenomenon of the "white trash" stereotype, with extensive material on the role of the hookworm campaign in redefining the Southern white working class.

Wright, Willard H. "Charles Wardell Stiles: 1867–1941." *The Journal of Parasitology* 27, no. 3 (June 1941): 195–201. A more formal biography of Stiles with good background on his early research on tapeworms.

Ziegler, Philip. *The Black Death.* Wolfeboro, NH: Sutton, 1991. A detailed account of the 14th century pandemic, with an emphasis on England. Well researched and authoritative but a bit dry.

Zinsser, Hans. *Rats, Lice and History.* Boston: Atlantic Monthly Press, 1935. The first great study of epidemic and vector-borne diseases, with an emphasis on typhus. Especially good for historical plagues.

Notes

Notes